Keepin' It Real

A Young Teen
Talks With God

Sandra McLeod Humphrey

CSS Publishing Company, Inc., Lima, Ohio

Library of Congress Cataloging-in-Publication Data

Humphrey, Sandra McLeod.
    Keepin' it real : a young teen talks with God / Sandra McLeod Humphrey.
        p. cm.
Summary: Through a series of letters to God from a shy teenage girl, explores such questions as "How important is prayer?", "What do you expect from God?", and "What does God expect from you?"
    ISBN 0-7880-1953-8 (pbk. : alk. paper)
    1. Teenage girls — Religious life. 2. Christian life. [1. Christian life.] I. Title.
    BV4551.3 H87 2003
    248.8'33—dc21
                                                                                                2002013718

For more information about CSS Publishing Company resources, visit our website at www.csspub.com or e-mail us at custserv@csspub.com or call (800) 241-4056.

ISBN 0-7880-1953-8   PRINTED IN U.S.A.

Dedicated to all the young men and women
with whom I have worked,
both professionally and as a volunteer.
You have taught me far more
than I could ever teach you.
Thank you!

Note To The Reader

Leslie has just turned thirteen and is having a very bad year. Not only is she stuck in a new school where she doesn't know anyone, but she is also stuck in a "life group" at her church where the leader of her small discussion group asks tough questions that she can't answer.

Questions like:

- How do you know that God is real in your life?
- When things go well, whom do you thank?
- When you have a problem, to whom do you turn for help?
- How important is prayer? Does God really answer our prayers?
- If God is a loving and caring God, why does he allow so many bad things to happen?
- What do you expect from God?
- What does God expect from you?

Come along and join Leslie on her faith journey as she begins to find answers to some of her questions.

Dear God,

I hope you don't mind if I write you a few letters now and then. Especially when I'm feeling down. Like right now.

I feel like I'm drowning and no one even knows I'm in the water. My whole world has changed: a new house, a new school, and even a new church.

Mom says that *you* never change. Well, I hope she's right because everything else in my life sure has changed.

I just found out I'm going to be stuck in what they call a "life group" at our new church. The group begins next week and I guess we're going to be talking about you a lot. I have no idea how many kids are going to be in the group, but it doesn't really matter because I'm not going to say anything anyway.

You know how shy I am. There's no way I'm going to talk about how I'm really feeling about anything to anyone. Especially to a bunch of kids I don't even know.

Tomorrow's the first day of school, so I guess I'd better go decide what I'm going to wear. Maybe I'll wear all black to match my mood. I think I like that idea a lot. I'd be making a statement about how I'm feeling. What do you think?

To be honest, I don't think anyone would even notice. Mom will be rushing around as usual, trying to get the kinks out of her hair, and Dad will have his head buried in his newspaper the way he always does in the morning. Sometimes it's like I'm invisible and no one even knows I'm here.

Tomorrow is going to be absolutely horrible. I can feel it in my bones. And no one even knows. Or cares. Do *you* care?

Maybe I'll talk to you again tomorrow. And then again, maybe I won't. I may not be in the mood to talk to anyone if my day turns out to be the disaster I think it's going to be.

Depressingly yours,
Leslie

Dear God,

I know I just wrote you a letter yesterday, but I have to talk to someone about how I'm feeling. I am so scared!

I've been dreading this day all summer. My first day at my new junior high. And now it's finally here.

I won't know a single soul in the whole school. Just think about that for a minute. If that isn't scary, I don't know what is.

And what if I can't find my classes? Or my locker? And what if I forget the combination to my lock? I've got it written down on a card in my backpack, but what if I lose the card?

And what if I have to eat lunch alone? Do you have any idea how embarrassing it is to eat lunch all by yourself? Talk about total humiliation!

And what if there aren't enough seats on the school bus and I have to stand up all the way to school? And all the way home?

I heard somewhere that there's a law that says that whatever can go wrong usually will go wrong, so I've got to tell you, I am most definitely expecting the worst. I just know today is going to be a total catastrophe.

Well, I guess I'm as ready as I'm ever going to be, so wish me luck. You know, I just thought of something. If I keep on writing, I might miss the bus and then I won't have to worry about the seats. But then Mom would just come all unglued and end up having to drive me to school and having your mom drive you to school would definitely not be cool. That would be even worse than having to stand up on the bus.

I guess I'd better bite the bullet and get out to the bus stop before things get any worse.

Fearfully and anxiously yours,
Leslie

P.S. Thanks for listening.

P.P.S. You *are* listening, aren't you?

Dear God,

Well, what did I tell you? I knew it was going to be an absolutely horrendous day and it was! If you have a few minutes, I'll tell you all the gruesome details. If my day were a movie, I think it would be rated "RRR" for really, really, really rotten!

Okay, are you ready, because here we go. First of all, I was late to my first class because I couldn't find room 221. Wouldn't you think 221 would be on the second floor? Well, it wasn't. It turned out to be a big home economics lab on the first floor just down the hall from 111. Now does that make any sense at all?

It doesn't to me either. I'm beginning to wonder if maybe the teachers hide the rooms on purpose just to make the new students look really dumb in front of the old students.

And you know how I told you that I wouldn't know anyone? It turned out to be even worse than I ever imagined. It seemed like everyone in the whole school knew everyone else and there I was all by my lonesome not knowing anyone. Boy, did I feel dumb. It sure seems that I'm feeling dumb a lot these days.

Everyone else was jabbering away like their meters would never run down and there I just sat all by myself, not knowing what to do. What I wanted to do was sink right through the floor and disappear from sight forever, but no such luck. I even closed my eyes and prayed that I would vaporize into nothingness. But when I opened my eyes, I was still there, so I just sat at my desk counting the dots on the girl's blouse in front of me.

By this time, I figured my day had to get better because it sure couldn't get any worse. Wrong! It did get worse, a thousand times worse.

At lunch I ended up sitting at a table all by myself looking dumb again. I could have just died! Boy, is that cafeteria huge. I just know that everyone in the whole place was staring at me, wondering what was wrong with me and why I didn't have any friends. Do you know what it's like to be an object of pity? Well, I can tell you, it's the pits and I may never eat in that cafeteria again. Ever.

To make a very long story short, my whole day went from horrible to horrendous until my last class, my gym class. Now I figured I finally had a chance to score something in the positive column because I love gym. I figured that maybe my day would at least end up okay. Wrong again!

I couldn't get the combination lock on my gym locker open. I tried three times and it just wouldn't open, so then the girl with the locker next to mine tried and she got it open the very first time. Boy, did I feel dumb! Again.

By the time I finally got my gym shorts and shirt on and got to class, they had already started playing volleyball. So there I sat all by myself in the bleachers, just watching and looking dumb again.

Boy, am I tired of looking and feeling dumb. The only good news is that at least I didn't miss the school bus and I made it home okay. There were plenty of seats, so I didn't have to stand up. But I think having all those empty seats actually made things worse because no one sat next to me. So there I was, sitting all by myself and looking dumb again.

So what do I do about tomorrow? There's no way I'm going to go through all that again. Do you know what it's like to feel really, really alone? Like you just don't fit in anywhere?

I'm sorry this letter got so long, but I just had to talk to someone after the rotten day I had. I'll try to keep my letters shorter in the future because I know you're busy too.

Frustratedly yours,
Leslie

Dear God,

It's me again. I actually made it through the first week of school and I have the battle scars to prove it.

I don't think I've told you about my math teacher yet. Mr. Jackson is a cross between Atilla the Hun and King Kong, and, believe me, I'm being kind.

He piles on the homework like his class is the only class we have and then during class he goes so fast that I can't even begin to keep up with him.

He tells us to ask questions if we don't understand something, but he goes so fast that I don't even know what I don't know until I get home and try to do the homework. So how does he expect me to ask a question when I'm stuck at home with his homework assignment and he's not even there?

I wonder if teachers get some kind of thrill out of going as fast as they can to see how far behind they can leave you. Maybe they even have some kind of secret club and the teacher who gets the kids the most confused and frustrated wins some kind of award from all the other teachers.

You know, that might make a great sci-fi movie. It could be about a teacher who pretends to want to help you but he really is trying to confuse you and make you so miserable that you end up dropping out of school.

I know, I know. Teachers really aren't like that, but sometimes it sure seems that they're not a whole lot of help, either.

I've really got to figure out what I'm going to do about this class before I end up failing it. I can't drop it because I need the math credits, but this is only the first week and I'm already drowning.

I figure if it goes on like this much longer, I won't even know what I thought I knew in the beginning before I started the class. I wonder if you can actually end up knowing less at the end of the year than you did at the beginning of the year. I think I'm about to find out.

Boy, no wonder some kids drop out of school. I'm not to that point yet, so don't worry. You'll be the first to know if I really start to go down the tubes.

I sure would like to tell Mom about some of this stuff, but she's so busy with the house that she just doesn't have time for me right now.

Did you see that stack of boxes in the garage that aren't even unpacked yet? It may take us all year just to get everything unpacked and put away.

I still haven't found Angelita. She's my favorite doll, the last thing Grandma Morgan gave me before she died. Mom is sure she's in one of those boxes and I sure hope she's right because I don't know what I would do if I lost Angelita. It would be like losing a little part of myself.

Speaking of losing things, I sure miss Grandma Morgan a lot. Maybe sometime we can talk about stuff like that. You know, dying and why people die when they do.

I don't think I'm up to it right now with this whole new school thing and everything, but there's a lot I don't understand about a lot of things, so maybe later when you have the time and I'm not so freaked out, we can talk about some of those things.

Right now I just want to forget all about my math class and Mr. Jackson, so I think I'll raid the refrigerator and drown myself in a hot fudge sundae.

Unmathematically yours,
Leslie

Wednesday, September 12

Dear God,

You are not going to believe this! I just got home from my first junior high life group at church and I still don't believe it myself.

First the pastor talks to us all in a big group which is just fine. I can handle that. I just have to sit there and I don't have to say anything if I don't want to. I don't even have to think if I don't want to.

But then we divide up into these small groups, so we can talk about things more privately. There are six other girls in my group, but they're not the problem either. The problem is our small group discussion leader. Her name is Ms. Wilson. She says we can call her Laurie, but I'll stick with "Ms. Wilson" if I stick at all.

I'm already thinking about dropping out of this group. Good grief, I'm just starting junior high. That's hassle enough. I definitely do not need this group.

Ms. Wilson tells us that anything we share in group won't leave the room and that if something is too personal to talk about, we don't have to talk about it. Yeah, right! I can just see what's coming already.

We're going to be expected to bare our souls in front of each other and there's no way I'm ever going to do that. Would you believe we're already talking about how we know you are real in our lives?

Good grief, I've never even thought about it. I say a quickie prayer every night, but I guess I kind of just say the usual stuff each time without thinking much about it. You know, like asking you to take care of everyone and that kind of stuff.

How do I know that you're real in my life? Beats me. I don't have a clue. Ms. Wilson wants us to think about that question all week and then we'll share some of our ideas next week.

She's got to be kidding! I don't even know these other girls yet. I'm sure not going to take a chance on saying something dumb in front of them. I already look dumb enough at school.

13

Speaking of school, one of the girls in my small group goes to my school and she's in my science class. Can't you just see what would happen if I say something dumb in the life group?

Cheryl will tell all her friends in our science class and then everyone will know that I'm even dumber than they thought I was. I know that everything we say in our small group is supposed to be confidential, but I don't really believe that for a minute, do you?

Well, I'm going to say my prayer and turn in because I'm really beat. We had to do so much thinking in that small group tonight that I'm like totally wiped out.

Maybe I'll add an extra line to my prayer tonight just to show you that I'm trying. Do my letters to you count? If they do, then maybe I'm off to a better start than I thought. Boy, this is all so confusing. Do you ever feel confused? Probably not.

Exhaustedly yours,
Your friend, Leslie

P.S. You know, everyone keeps telling me to enjoy these years because these are the good years, the fun years. Who do they think they're kidding? I'm already so stressed out that I don't even want to think about tomorrow. I don't even want to think about today!

Friday, September 14

Dear God,

I just knew it! I'm the shortest one in my class again. Remember, I told you I would be and I don't think you believed me. Well, I knew I would be and I am. I always am and I probably always will be for the rest of my entire life.

The only good news here is that at least I don't have to deal with all those dumb old jokes about being "vertically challenged." So far no one's even talking to me yet, let alone cracking any jokes.

You know, it's really strange how everyone else just seems to sprout up over the summer. Everyone but me. Some girls are even complaining about being too tall. Can you imagine?

Boy, I would trade them just about anything I have for just a couple of their inches. Mom is always telling me to look on the bright side of things. So what's the bright side of being a midget? If you think of something good, be sure to let me know because I've been thinking about it for a lot of years now and I can tell you there is no bright side to being the shortest kid in the world.

I always get stuck in the front row in all my classes, so the teachers are sure I can see the blackboard. Just once I'd like to sit in the back row and see what goes on in the rest of the world. I just know that's where all the action is, in the last row.

And do you know what it's like to be the shortest kid when the other kids are choosing up a basketball team? You guessed it. Pain city! I'm always the last to get picked and I always have the feeling that I should apologize to whoever gets stuck with me.

Believe me, there is no bright side to being short. If there were one, I would have discovered it by now because I've sure been looking.

Well, I've got to go. Mom needs someone small to crawl under the back porch and find the nozzle to the hose which somehow rolled under there. See what I mean? There is no bright side.

Bye for now,
Your short friend, Leslie

P.S. If there are any snakes under there, I'll be out of there faster than you can say Rumplestiltskin.

15

Dear God,

Well, I've got good news and I've got bad news. Which do you want to hear first?

I think I'll start with the bad news, so that I can end with the good news. I think it's important to end with an upper whenever you can, don't you?

The bad news is that they didn't cancel our life group tonight. If you remember, I asked you to seriously consider figuring out some way to get the group canceled, but I guess you weren't listening because it didn't get canceled and Ms. Wilson was there for our small group discussion.

Now for the good news. You know how I've always wondered if you really hear all our prayers? And how I've been wondering why sometimes you answer them and sometimes you don't. Well, I think I'm beginning to figure it out.

In our large group, before we went off to our small groups, Pastor Hardy gave each one of us a puzzle piece and asked us to describe the puzzle. Well, of course, no one could because we each just had one small piece and one piece doesn't tell you very much about the whole puzzle.

So then in our small groups we talked about living each day by faith with just our one puzzle piece, not knowing what the whole puzzle is eventually going to look like since we can't see the whole puzzle yet. But we know that *you* can see the whole puzzle because you always see the larger picture instead of just the little bit that we see.

You know, I think that makes a lot of sense. Obviously, since you can see everything, you're always looking at the larger picture instead of coming all unglued over all the nitty-gritty details the way the rest of us do.

You can probably tell I don't have it all figured out yet, but I think I'm beginning to get it. I'll just have to think about it some more on my own time.

Then we talked about how we know you are real in our lives and whether or not you answer our prayers. I thought it was kind of weird that we were talking about prayers since I had just asked you to cancel our class and obviously you hadn't been listening.

Well, it turns out that maybe I was wrong. Everyone in our small group gave examples of how you have answered a lot of their prayers. I didn't say anything since I was still thinking about the fact that you had ignored my prayer and obviously hadn't been listening to me.

But then Ms. Wilson asked us if we had ever prayed prayers that hadn't been answered and, since everyone else raised their hands, I raised my hand too.

Then we got into a whole big discussion about whether you always answer prayers or not. I was thinking that when you didn't answer my prayers the way I wanted you to that you weren't listening, but I think maybe I was wrong about that.

We ended up talking about that larger picture and how you see a lot of things that we don't see. What we finally decided is that you *always* hear our prayers and you *always* answer our prayers, but sometimes your answer is "No" or "Not yet" because you can see that larger picture that we can't see.

Ms. Wilson gave an example of a mother taking her little boy shopping and he wants this cheap little toy car that his mom knows is going to fall apart the first time he plays with it. And she also knows that he is getting a brand new red tricycle next week for his birthday, so she doesn't buy him the cheap toy he wants now since she knows he will be getting something a lot better very soon.

Of course, he doesn't understand why he can't have the cheapie toy when he wants it because he doesn't understand the difference between the good stuff and the bad stuff yet, but his mom knows and so she does what she thinks is best for him in the long run.

I think I can see where Ms. Wilson was going with this because I know that you are a loving father who knows what is best for us too, even when we may not know ourselves. Like that time I wanted that cheap skateboard and my dad wouldn't buy it for me because he didn't think it was safe. Then two months later it got recalled. I guess sometimes we just have to trust, don't we?

You know, our discussion tonight made me feel a lot better because now that I'm sure you really are listening, I think I'll feel more like praying. Real prayers, not just the little quickie prayers I've been doing most of my life.

Well, anyway, that's the good news. We'll be talking a lot more about how we know you are real in our lives. I think I'm almost looking forward to those talks now that I know they're not going to be as scary as I thought they were going to be.

I may not drop out of this group after all.

Optimistically yours,
Your friend, Leslie

P.S. I think I'm going to really try talking to you tonight when I say my prayer. You know, talk to you from my heart and not just from my head. Maybe I'll begin by talking to you about Mom and Dad and see how that goes.

P.P.S. I just can't tell you how glad I am to know that you are really listening.

Dear God,

Good grief, here we go again! I just had lecture #1001 from Dad about the importance of being a "team player" and now I think I'm getting an Excedrin headache #6000.

Well, that will teach me to keep my big mouth shut when I have a problem. You know how this all started? I was stuck playing left field again today in our softball game. In case you didn't know, left field is a strictly nowhere position reserved for those kids the coach doesn't like.

I really wanted to play first base again like I did last year at my old school, but Mr. Evans gave first base to a really drippy kid who's always slobbering all over him, telling him how great he is. I can't believe she's for real, but then I can't believe Mr. Evans is for real either. He must be a real yo-yo if he actually falls for all that garbage she's giving him.

Well, anyway, I was feeling really down about being stuck out in left field where there's no action at all and the only living thing I ever see is an occasional lost butterfly. So there I was in the kitchen telling Mom how unfair the whole thing is when Dad pops in and immediately gets on my case for not being a team player.

You probably know his whole routine yourself by now. How you should be happy to play whatever position the coach gives you as long as "it's for the good of the team" and how "every position is important." I got the same lecture last year when I wanted to drop out of my drama class because I always got stuck painting the scenery with all those dumb sunflowers and squirrels instead of doing any acting. Do you realize that I never did get a role all year? All I got from that class was tennis elbow and a bent back from always being bending over painting something dumb.

I've learned one thing though. When Dad's on one of his "team player" crusades, there's no point in even trying to discuss the matter with him, so it looks like I'm probably going to be stuck out in left field forever.

You know what else he said? He told me I should try working myself up to a better position by showing the coach what I can do.

Do you believe that? How can I prove anything to the coach when I'm standing out there in No Man's Land just watching the old butterflies and dandelions?

Talk about being unreal — I don't think parents are much better than coaches sometimes. Not counting you, of course. I bet you were a great dad. I bet you were a good listener too and didn't always try to tell everyone what to do.

Sometimes I get so frustrated that I feel like leaving home. But who would take care of all my stuffed animals then? And who would feed Max?

Speaking of Max, did I ever thank you for getting my parents to finally see how important getting a dog was to me? It took two years, but it was worth the wait. I will remember last Valentine's Day forever.

As soon as we got to the Animal Shelter, I knew right away that Max was my dog. The card on his cage said "Maximilian," but I just called him Max right from the start.

Do you remember how he snuggled up to me right away and cried when he thought I was going to leave him there? And do you remember how Dad complained that he was too big and Mom had to convince him that "big was good" and that Max would make a wonderful watch dog?

Mom was right. Max has turned out to be a great dog. He's almost a year old now and he's ninety pounds of love all rolled into a huge mound of black fluffy fur.

You know how people talk about "unconditional love" all the time? That's how Max loves me. He doesn't care if I'm short or skinny or have mousy brown hair. He doesn't even care if I'm shy and don't have a lot of friends.

Is that how you love me too? That's really pretty cool to be loved like that.

Well, I think I'm feeling a little better now, so I may as well go start on my homework.

Less dismally yours,
Your friend, Leslie

Dear God,

I hope you weren't watching our gym class today. But if you were, then you saw our new gym shorts. Now everyone can see how skinny my legs are.

That means I can't wear my old shorts anymore. I really liked those shorts because they came down to my knees and no one could see how skinny my thighs are.

Now that we're stuck having to wear these new gym shorts, there's no way I can hide my thighs and I just know that some kid is going to start calling me "toothpicks."

You're probably beginning to think that all I ever do is complain, but you're the only one I really have to talk to, so I guess that's why you get to hear all the bad stuff.

Speaking of bad stuff, did I tell you that Mrs. Anderson, the principal, is threatening to make our whole school wear uniforms? I guess she doesn't like some of the logos the kids have on their shirts, but don't you think making all of us wear uniforms is a little extreme?

Or maybe not! If we wore uniforms, then I wouldn't have to spend so much time trying to decide what to wear every day. I guess I'll have to give that some serious thought before I decide whether or not to add uniforms to my worry list.

Okay, are you ready for a real "upper"? Last night was my life group and I've got to tell you, I think I almost enjoyed it. In our large group, we got blank sheets of paper taped to our backs and then we just wandered around the room while people wrote things about us on our paper. Like I wrote "laughs a lot" on one boy's back and I wrote "has pretty hair" on Cheryl's back.

You're not going to believe this, but someone wrote "very smart" and someone else wrote "pretty" on my paper. Then there were other things like "quiet" and "nice" and "sensitive" and some other ones too, but can you believe that someone actually wrote "pretty" on my paper? I wonder if it was a boy or a girl who wrote that. I'll probably never find out, but I know one thing. I'm going to save that piece of paper forever.

Well, anyway, after our large group, we went off to our small groups as usual. We always start off our small groups by sharing a little about how our week has gone before we begin our regular discussion, but last night we never got to our regular discussion at all.

One of the girls was so upset about not making the cheerleading squad at her school that she actually started to cry while she was telling us about it. Her name is Becky and she's convinced that she didn't make the cheerleading squad because she's so "homely." That's her word, not mine.

She's sitting there telling us how her eyes are too small and her nose is too big and how she's just got to lose at least twenty pounds.

And I'm sitting there thinking this girl is really crazy. I don't think her nose is too big at all. I think it gives her face character. And her eyes are beautiful. They're dark brown just like her hair and I think they're just the right size. And if she lost twenty pounds, she'd look like an X-ray.

I know I complain a lot about my skinny legs and being too short, but my legs really are too skinny and I really am too short. But Becky is really beautiful and she doesn't even know it.

I guess she just doesn't see herself the way the rest of us see her. That really makes you think, doesn't it? You know, about why she sees herself so differently from the way we see her.

Well, anyway, instead of getting into our regular lesson, we read Psalm 100 which tells us that it is you who made us and that we didn't make ourselves. And then Cheryl added that you don't make any junk. Even Becky smiled when Cheryl said that.

Then we went on to Psalm 139 which tells us that we are "fearfully and wonderfully made" and how wonderful all your works are. Now I've got to tell you, it kind of changes your thinking when we're reminded that each of us is a special creation made by you and that no one is exactly like anyone else.

It kind of makes a person feel special, like maybe there's a reason why you made us the way you made us. I think maybe we're getting back to that "larger picture" again. How maybe you know what's best for us even when sometimes we don't.

Our group meets in the church library and that library got so quiet that you could have heard a popsicle melt. I think we were all thinking about those verses we had just read and doing some really serious contemplating.

It's kind of like if someone gives you a special gift and you just blow it away like it's not worth anything and you don't even appreciate it or say, "Thank you."

We talked a lot more and then we all agreed that if you make each of us a unique creation, then that makes each of us very special. So we're going to try thanking you for making us the way you made us, instead of always finding fault with ourselves for not looking exactly the way we want to look. I have a hunch that no one is really ever totally satisfied with the way they look.

I know girls who I think are too skinny, but they think they're too fat and I know boys who think they're too tall, but I think they're just right. This is taking me a long time to say this, but I kind of had to figure it out while I was writing it down.

I think from now on I'm going to complain less about how I look and just figure that you know what you're doing and that eventually I'll look the way I'm supposed to look.

I still can't believe someone actually wrote "pretty" on my paper. Boy, I sure wish I knew who it was or maybe it's better if I don't know who wrote it. This way, every time I look at one of the other kids, I can think that maybe that's the kid who wrote it and that will make me feel good toward that other kid. Really good.

Well, I'd better go set the table for dinner, but aren't you glad that things are going so well in my life group?

Blushingly yours,
Your friend, Leslie

P.S. I think I've figured out how to solve the problem with my combination lock on my gym locker. I'll just never lock my locker. After all, who would want to steal my gym shorts?

Dear God,

Here we go again! Parents can be so unreasonable. It's bad enough not having any friends, but now my parents won't even let me adopt two little white rats.

I've got this once-in-a-lifetime chance to get these two really great rats from this kid at school for only a dollar each and I will never have another chance like this ever again.

His mom is making him get rid of them because he forgot to lock their cage last night and the whole family had to hunt all over the house for them this morning. Well, it was really no big deal because they finally found them in his mom's closet all curled up in her furry bedroom slippers, but he says that she probably hasn't stopped screaming yet.

Anyway, the kid's mom refused to let the rats remain in the house another day, so he had to bring them to school this morning. And now they're just sitting there in the science lab, waiting for someone to adopt them and take them home.

Mr. Bennett is a nice guy, but he isn't going to let those guys stay in his lab forever. It must be terrible not to have a real home and to feel that nobody wants you.

I know they have each other, so it's not like they're totally alone or anything, but who wants to live their life in a science lab?

I told my parents I'd pay for the rat food myself, I'd keep their cage cleaned out, and I'd be sure their cage was always locked so that they couldn't get out. But no deal! Both Mom and Dad refuse to let the rats come home. They both agree that white rats are just not their idea of a house pet and that Max is enough pet for any house. Well, at least they agree on that. They sure don't agree on much else anymore.

Remember how you softened my parents up so that I could get Max? Do you think you could do that again? These rats really need a home and they need it fast.

I know just how those guys feel. When you don't feel you belong, it's like being on a whole different planet and you don't have a clue as to what you should do to try to "fit in." No one else even seems to know you're alive and even your own parents just don't seem to notice how unhappy you are.

Well, I've got to go — Dad is calling me. I wonder what I've done wrong now.

Unhappily yours,
Your lonely friend, Leslie

P.S. Do you think my parents would change their mind about those rats if I told them I was thinking of becoming a biologist and that depriving me of those rats could irrevocably damage my future career?

P.P.S. My life group got canceled this week because of a conference, and you know what? I think I actually miss that group. I wonder what that means. It probably just means that I must be getting pretty desperate if I miss Ms. Wilson.

Dear God,

Well, here I am again. Did you miss me? I'm sorry I haven't written for a while, but I've been busy reading this book about positive thinking. Some of it sounds kind of corny, but I think I might give it a try anyway.

This book repeats itself a lot. In fact, I think the guy who wrote it could have said everything he has to say in ten pages instead of a 110. But then, who would buy a ten-page book?

I guess the main thing I'm getting out of the book is that I really don't have any problems. Problems are really only "challenges" and "opportunities." He says that if you have the right attitude, you can meet any challenge and solve any problem. He even says that solving problems and meeting challenges can be fun. He must be a little whacko himself or he'd know that having problems is never any fun.

I really don't know about this guy. He may be some kind of weirdo who's never had a problem and is just making all this stuff up so he can write a book and get rich quick.

Did you know that all people who write books get rich? I heard that somewhere. I wonder if it's true. If it is, then maybe I'll write a book too.

Maybe all this positive thinking stuff is just some kind of fancy hocus-pocus to get you to buy his book so he can get rich, but I figure I'll give it a try. Some of the stuff just might work and, besides, what do I have to lose?

Is it okay if we get serious for a few minutes? I've got another problem. Another "challenge." And I don't know exactly what to do.

You know that I've believed in you for my whole life or at least for as long as I can remember. But there are some kids in my class who think it's dumb to believe that there's really a God. They don't seem to believe in anything.

They ask some pretty good questions that there just don't seem to be any answers for. At least, I don't have any answers for those questions.

They ask questions like: If you are real, then why do you let all those children in Rwanda starve to death? And why do you let some of our own people die so painfully from cancer? And why do you let our crime rate keep going up? And why don't you help all those unemployed people find jobs? And why do you let some babies be born deformed or retarded?

Well, anyway, you get the idea. They've got a point. So why do you?

I know one thing for sure. It's important that I know whether or not you are real, so I'm just going to have to find out for myself. For a while there I was absolutely sure that you were real and I was sure that you listened to all our prayers. But now I'm not sure exactly what I believe.

I don't want to hurt your feelings or anything, but I really do have to find out for myself that you are real, so what do I do?

Maybe I'll just have to keep talking to you and see what happens. I know you won't be talking to me in regular words, but it's really, really important that you do let me know somehow that you are real.

Confusedly yours,
Your friend, Leslie

P.S. You know how I've been complaining all this time because no one talks to me? Well, now there arc two kids who *are* actually talking to me. Kevin puts me down a lot and teases me, but Jasmine really seems to care about what I think and she even asked me to eat lunch at her table yesterday. So I want to thank you for getting two people to actually talk to me. I may not be a social butterfly or anything, but at least this is a pretty good beginning, don't you think?

Dear God,

I hate to sound like a real square, but I'm worried about these two guys in my class. They sneak off during their free period every day to do whatever they do and come back all zoned out for the rest of the day.

You know what I don't understand? All the other kids know these guys are using and all the teachers must know they're using, so why doesn't someone do something about it?

Mrs. Anderson is threatening to make us all wear uniforms if we don't start sticking to the dress code, but what about the drugs and the booze? It's like this school is sweating bullets over the little stuff and just ignores the really important stuff.

In my old school, kids were kicked out of school just for lighting up a plain old cigarette, but at this school there seems to be some kind of unwritten code that says even if you know what's going on, you keep your mouth shut and you don't rat on anyone.

I would think it would be very scary if you thought that no one really cared about you. Sometimes I feel like that, but I know in my heart of hearts that my mom and dad do care.

Remember how Dad threatened to ground me for a month if I even smoked a regular cigarette? He'd probably ground me for life if I tried something really X-rated.

I think maybe some kids use drugs just to see if anyone really cares enough to try to stop them. Do you think I'm way off base on this? Maybe I am, but I think it's really important that kids know that someone cares about them.

Boy, this letter got pretty heavy, didn't it? I didn't mean to get so serious, but this drug thing really bothers me and so far you're the only one I can talk to about it. I wonder if maybe we could talk about some of this stuff in my life group. I'll have to think about that.

Wait a minute, hold everything! I think there *is* some good news. You know how I've always told you that I wished boys had never been invented? Well, maybe I've changed my mind. Just maybe. There's this boy at school who's got his locker next to mine. His name's Brandon and I think he just might be okay.

So far I haven't worked up the nerve to say anything to him but maybe tomorrow.

First, I've got to figure out what to say. You may not understand just how important first impressions are, but they are very, very important, so I'll have to choose my first words very carefully.

Maybe just a quick "hi." That way, if he doesn't say anything to me, I can just cover my mouth and pretend I'm sneezing or yawning or coughing or something. What do you think?

Or maybe you think I should take a more direct approach and just say something straight out like, "Hey, I see you've got the locker next to mine." Or would that just be stating the obvious and he might think I'm even dumber than he probably already thinks I am?

How about if I pretend to have trouble getting my locker open? Do you think he might offer to help? You probably think that's pretty tacky, right? Yeah, I think so too. I don't think that's the way to go.

I think this is going to take a whole lot more planning than I thought, so if you have any good ideas, be sure to let me know. I'll try anything within reason even if it only has half a chance of working. In fact, maybe I'll even try something that's *not* within reason.

Well, I've got to go. I can hear Dad's car in the driveway and I haven't raked the leaves yet, so I've got to make it out to the backyard before he gets there and sees that I haven't even started yet.

Busily yours,
Your friend, Leslie

Dear God,

Did you hear that door just slam? If I'd done that, I would have been grounded for a year.

That was Mom. She just saw my room! Why can't she just accept the fact that everyone's an individual and that we all have different ideas about what "clean" means?

Everything on my dresser is stuff I use every day, so why should I put it away? That would just waste a lot of time and then I wouldn't have as much time to spend doing the really important things. Like listening to my CDs and planning my strategy for that boy who's got his locker next to mine at school.

She finally agreed that I could leave some of the things on top of my dresser. But then she got really picky and started checking my bookshelves. Except for that book on positive thinking, I don't read much, so why should I keep books on my bookshelves? That kind of thinking is pretty rigid, if you ask me.

Besides, I need those shelves for all my important stuff, the stuff she calls "junk." I don't think it's right that she calls some of my stuff "junk" just because it doesn't seem important or valuable to her, do you?

How about that little plastic box she keeps in her top dresser drawer which she doesn't even know I know about? You know what she keeps in there? The wrapper from a piece of chewing gum, a little piece of white netting, a valentine from me when I was in kindergarten, and a whole bunch of other stuff.

Now doesn't that just seem like a lot of junk if you don't know the memories that go with each thing? Like that chewing-gum wrapper was from the gum my dad gave her on their very first date — his very first gift to her, if you can call a stick of gum a gift.

And that little piece of white netting she cut from her bridal veil before she gave her wedding dress and her veil away to her cousin in Alabama. Now I ask you, if you didn't know that piece of white netting was from her bridal veil, wouldn't you just think that was a piece of junk?

So what I'm saying here is that I don't think anyone else should decide what is "junk" because what might look like junk to one person could have some really wonderful memories for the other person.

Actually, I think I might have convinced her to let me keep my stuff on my bookshelves if she hadn't looked under my bed.

So what else would I keep under my bed except my cassettes, my CDs, and my dirty clothes? She's lucky I don't keep my dirty dishes under there like some kids I know.

And it's not as if *all* my dirty clothes were there! It just depends where I am at the time. Some of my dirty clothes are on the floor of my closet and some of them are stuffed into my dresser drawers.

Well, anyway, that's when she told me that was the "last straw" and went storming out of my room, slamming the door after her.

Just before she lost her cool and stormed out of my room, she asked me how I expected her to vacuum under my bed. Well, I don't. I don't vacuum under it, so why should she? After all, who ever looks under your bed except your mother?

Well, I'd better go. I want to fix up my room before Dad gets home so that, when Mom shows him my room, he won't understand why she's so upset.

Talk to you later,

Not-so-tidily yours,
Your friend, Leslie

P.S. I'm lucky Mom didn't look in my drawers or she would have really blown a fuse.

P.P.S. Do you think she'd get really sneaky and show Dad my drawers? You're right, I'd better work on them too.

P.P.P.S. You know, when you get right down to the basics, why should I even have to make my bed? I'm just going to mess it up again every night. Talk about a real waste of time — that is really a totally nonsensical job if there ever was one. After all, who in the world really cares if my bed is made? You see what I mean about having to decide for yourself what's really important? Otherwise, you could end up wasting your entire life just doing dumb things which have no real meaning or true significance.

P.P.P.P.S. I just want to thank you again for always being there for me. I don't think there's anyone else in the whole world I could talk to the way I talk to you.

Dear God,

You know what? I think I'm finally catching on to some of that "positive thinking" stuff. And if it works for me, it must work for anyone.

So far I've managed to make one new friend by taking the first step and saying something positive to a girl in my home room. I'm not going to tell you what I said to her because it was pretty dumb, but anyway it must have worked because after I said something positive to her, we both just started talking and we discovered that we both loved Disney movies and rollerblading and a whole bunch of other things.

Megan may not be the prettiest or the brainiest or the most popular girl in my class, but that's okay because I'm not either.

You know what I think I'll try next? You remember that boy who has his locker next to mine? I think I'm almost ready to make my first move. I'm not exactly sure just yet what my first move will be, but I can feel I'm getting close.

You're probably wondering how my life group has been going since I haven't talked much about it lately. It's been going okay, but I've been doing a lot of heavy thinking and that's why I haven't mentioned the group.

We've been talking a lot about some of those questions the kids at school are asking. You know, about why bad things happen if you are really a loving God. I think I'm beginning to get it figured out. Maybe not all of it, but at least some of it.

It seems to me the bottom line here is that you made a perfect world for us because you loved us and wanted us to be happy. The Bible tells us that you were pleased with everything you created and I think you were, but then you had a big choice to make.

Should you keep everything perfect just the way it was or should you give us free will and let us make our own decisions and our own choices, knowing we would probably mess up if you did let us make our own choices?

If you don't give us free will, then you know everything will remain perfect and we'll stay close to you and we won't mess up.

But if you *do* give us free will, you know we're bound to mess up and we just might drift away from you to do our own thing, whatever that is.

I think that must have been a really tough decision for you, but I think you decided to give us free will because you loved us so much that you wanted us to come to you on our own and actually make that choice for ourselves. Kind of like when we choose to do something right when we're tempted to do something wrong. Deciding for ourselves what we're going to do makes it that much more special and important.

I've been thinking a lot about this and I think that by giving us free will, that actually strengthens our relationship to you because we're choosing to believe in you or not to believe in you for ourselves. And when we choose to believe in you, that makes our relationship a lot more special and meaningful.

I still think that must have been a really hard decision for you though, knowing we were bound to mess up big-time. When we let our greed or our jealousy get the best of us and we do dumb things that get us in trouble, I'm sure that hurts you, but you promised to stick by us even when we do dumb things. I think that's pretty cool.

When you really think about it, I think we cause a lot of our own problems. Like all the violence in the world and all the ecology problems and all the diseases like AIDS and cancer. I think if we took better care of the earth and thought more before we did stuff, we probably wouldn't have all the problems we have.

I'll probably have to keep thinking about this stuff because there's a lot to figure out, but I think I'm on the right track. I think "moderation" figures in all this somewhere too, but I'm just beginning to work on that. You know, doing things moderately instead of to excess. Like eating or buying stuff or even sex. I think it probably all comes down in the end to using our common sense and good judgment which we all have, but we don't always use.

Aren't you surprised that I'm figuring so much stuff out? By the way, you know how I was beginning to wonder if you're really out there? Well, I'm almost convinced for sure that you are. Maybe not 100 percent yet, but I think if I keep on track, then I'll know for sure pretty soon.

I can hear Mom calling me, so I'd better go. She probably wants me to help her make the spaghetti. I would never tell anyone else, but my spaghetti is really a lot better than hers. My secret is the garlic. I just love garlic, don't you?

Positively yours,
Your friend, Leslie

P.S. You know, actually I have two friends now because I still eat lunch with Jasmine at her table and I also do a lot of stuff with Megan. I wonder if they would like each other. Maybe sometime we can all do something together. I think that could be pretty cool, don't you?

P.P.S. You remember those two boys in my class I was telling you about who were using? I heard that they're both at some treatment center now, so I guess maybe I was wrong about Mrs. Anderson. I guess she does care about the kids.

Saturday, November 24

Dear God,

Well, I just finished breakfast, but I'm not real sure just what I had. Mom's on some new health food kick and so now I never know what I'm eating.

Have you ever eaten *green* blueberry muffins? Probably not. Well, I just did and now I know why they're green. It's because Mom mixes spirulina in the batter and it turns everything green. *Yuck!*

You probably know all about spirulina, but all I know is that it's some kind of seaweed or algae or something and that's all I need to know. Sometimes it's better not to know too much, if you know what I mean.

Now here's another one for you. I bet you don't know what's inside the meat loaf I've been eating and thought I liked until now. Are you ready for this one? Oatmeal, wheat germ, and bran. Can you imagine? Some people will stop at nothing! Why can't she just make regular meat loaf with bread crumbs the way other mothers do?

And you know the fried zucchini I told you about the other night? I thought it was really yummy at the time. Well, I guess it wasn't as yummy as I thought it was. You know what she used for the batter to fry it in? Wheat germ! That is really sick!

Well, I know one thing. I'm not eating another thing in this house again without inspecting it *very* carefully.

And now she's got all of us taking vitamins. We're taking vitamins to improve our vision, vitamins to prevent colds, minerals for our bones and teeth, and now she's even got us taking garlic capsules. Don't ask me why we're taking garlic capsules because I don't know why and I don't think I even want to know why. All I know is that they'd better not leave me with bad breath because I have enough problems already. Garlic in spaghetti sauce is one thing. Garlic in a capsule is something else entirely.

Did you hear Mom calling me? She wanted to know when I'm going to dust the living room and put the dishes in the dishwasher away.

Nag, nag, nag, that's all parents ever do. They're always telling me all the things I do that are wrong. Why don't they ever tell me about some of the things that I do right?

Last night they got all bent out of shape over my money. I repeat, *my* money. They were upset because I couldn't remember where the ten dollars I got for babysitting Mrs. Tozer's twins went. I know that "money does not grow on trees." They've told me enough times, so that it is burned into my brain forever.

I know I spent some of the money on my movie magazine, but I'm just not sure where the rest went. Why do they need to know anyway? After all, it's my money, not theirs. I earned it, they didn't.

Then they wanted to know where my allowance went. Good grief, I don't know where it went. I earned it doing some of those dumb jobs around the house that no one else wants to do and I shouldn't have to account for every penny I earn anyway.

Now they're threatening to put me on a budget. More rules, always more rules. A budget is a list you make of all the necessities you have to spend your money on so that you don't have any money left over for the fun stuff. They're even telling me it's time I learned to start saving a little each week so that I can open my own savings account at the bank.

They've got to be kidding! I can hardly scrape by on what I earn now. How do they expect me to *save* anything? I'd like to see them try saving on what I earn a week.

You know what I'm going to do? I'm going to start making a list of all my grievances. Grievances are the things I don't like because they're not fair. Then, when I'm a parent, I'll look at my list, and I'll know what to do and what not to do.

Don't you think that's a good idea? You can even help me when you have time if you want to. I can tell you one thing; I'm going to be one super terrific parent because I won't make all the dumb mistakes my parents are always making.

I'll get back to you after I finish my list.

Indebtedly yours,
Your friend, Leslie

37

P.S. Speaking of money, that reminded me of something Pastor Hardy was telling us Wednesday night. He was talking about "tithing" and how important it is. I guess I'm supposed to give you ten percent of whatever I make to help people who don't have as much as I do. He also told us that unless we give our tithe with a cheerful heart, it won't mean very much. Actually, I like that idea a lot! I think I would feel really good giving money to help other people — like that family on the TV news last night who lost everything in a fire. Maybe I'll begin by sending something to that family. And I always give something to Santa Anonymous every year. Does that count? Maybe I'll make a list of some of the people I want to give my money to. I think sharing is good, don't you?

Dear God,

Well, today I have some good news and I have some bad news. Which do you want to hear first?

I think I'll give you the good news first. The good news is that today the braces came off my teeth and they look great (my teeth, that is, not the braces).

The bad news is that the rest of me is still the same. My nose is still too flat, my eyes are still too small, I still have a flat chest, and I'm still the shortest one in my class.

Mom is always telling me that my eyes are beautiful and not to worry about my flat chest. She says to just give it enough time and it'll develop. I sure hope she's right. What if I'm still flat-chested after I'm all through growing? Who would want a flat-chested girl-friend? It could wreck my entire life!

Actually, when you think about it, everything about me is flat. Even my nose. I've tried squeezing my nose together with my fingers whenever I have nothing better to do. So far my nose still looks the same, but I think maybe now my fingers look a little flatter too. Sometimes all that happens is that my nose gets all stuffed up and I have trouble breathing, but that's okay. I don't mind not breathing for a while if my nose will look better in the end.

I don't know for sure, but I think maybe some people luck out with beauty and some people luck out with brains, but I'm also thinking that maybe some people don't luck out with much of anything.

Oh, well, at least now I have great-looking teeth. Did you notice the beginning of my new positive attitude? After all, teeth are important too. And besides, I can't forget that you made each of us special. You made us just the way you wanted us, so there must be some reason you wanted me to be so flat. Maybe some day you'll tell me.

Say, do you remember that boy I was telling you about? The one with the locker next to mine? Well, I just realized this morning that he's in my math class. I always have so much trouble trying to keep up with Mr. Jackson when he's drawing all that stuff on the blackboard that I've never had time to look around and see who else is in the class.

But he's there all right. I was rushing to class today and I just barely made it through the door as the bell rang. As I made a dive for my desk, I tripped over a pair of legs sticking out in the aisle. Well, you can just guess who those legs belonged to. Boy, he sure must have long legs. Most kids just keep their legs under their desks where they they belong, but maybe his won't fit.

Well, anyway, as I was picking up my books, I saw him watching me. Yeah, yeah, I know what you're thinking. So why didn't he help me pick up my books? Good grief, I don't know. At least he didn't laugh hysterically like everyone else in the class.

Besides, maybe he's shy like me. Do you know why I think maybe he's shy? Because toward the end of class I think he was looking at me again. I'm not sure he was looking at me because I was afraid to look up and check, but you know how sometimes you can just feel when someone's watching you and I really think he was.

I think I'm almost ready to make my move now. So what do you think? If you have ideas, let me know because I don't want to waste any more valuable time if I can help it.

Please get back to me as soon as you can on this.

Hopefully yours,
Your friend, Leslie

Dear God,

Good news! You *are* real. And you hear me! You know how I've been talking to you? Not just my quickie little prayers but really talking. How I just started talking to you about my problems and how I really wanted you to let me know that you were listening.

And then I just kept on talking to you more and more. Just like you were my best friend. Actually you *were* my best friend. My *only* friend.

I just had to know for myself if you were real and I've got to tell you, you came through with flying colors. You know, it's funny how you did everything.

You didn't exactly answer me the way I thought you were going to, but each time you did answer me in such a way that I knew for sure that you heard me.

Like in the beginning, I asked you to make me really popular and give me lots of friends. Well, you gave me *one* friend. That was Jasmine. And then a little bit later, you gave me another friend, Megan.

Jasmine and I still eat lunch together almost every day and Megan and I have gone to two movies together and this weekend we're going to a pizza party together. I'm still thinking that sometime soon I'll get all three of us to do something together. I think Jasmine and Megan would like each other and I think it's important to share friends, don't you?

And remember how I asked you to take away all my problems because I was feeling overloaded with so much stuff to worry about? So you didn't take away my problems, but you helped me find that book on positive thinking which is helping me deal with the problems I have.

You know, I think everyone has problems and I don't think it's your job to take away our problems, but I think I'm beginning to believe your promise that you'll always be there for us to help us with our problems.

I could go on and on, but you probably get the idea. Every time I asked for help, I got it, but not exactly in the way I expected to get it. I think that's part of that "larger picture" Ms. Wilson is always talking about.

She says that you know what we need before we even ask for it and that you also know what's best for us in the long run, so I guess it comes down to a matter of trust. Either I'm going to trust you or I'm not, and I've decided that I *am* going to trust you to always be there for me and to help me through the tough times.

Now that I know for myself that you are real, no one can tell me any different. I know what I know and if anyone else wants to know if you are really real, then they should do what I did and just try talking to you too.

I think this is what Ms. Wilson means when she's always telling us that to have a really close personal relationship with you, we have to talk to you a lot. She says "pray" a lot, but I think what she really means is just talk to you a lot. She says it's like any relationship. The more we talk to someone, the more we get to know them and the more we learn to trust them. I never thought I'd ever say this, but I think I'm beginning to like Ms. Wilson.

You know, at first I thought you might be too busy with bigger and more important things to pay any attention to me and my problems, but now I know that you're never too busy for any of us. I guess you're just like any good mother or father — just waiting for us to talk to you and tell you how we really feel about things.

Ms. Wilson says that the Bible tells us that you care so much about everyone and everything you created that you even keep track of every sparrow and you've even numbered every hair on our heads. Boy, I think that's totally awesome!

I've got to tell you, this is really a big load off my mind, knowing there's someone out there I can always count on. I feel so much better now! This means that now I know I have someone who will always be there for me.

Hold on a minute while I go see what Dad wants. When he calls me *Leslie* instead of "Les," it's usually bad news, so cross your fingers and I'll be right back.

Oh, boy, here we go again! Dad just saw my report card and I guess I've committed the unpardonable sin. I got a *C* in math. So what's wrong with a *C* anyway? I know lots of kids who got *D*s and *F*s.

I don't know how much you know about our math, but I can tell you it's nothing like it used to be. Now it's so hard that even our parents can't help us with our homework anymore.

And they're complaining about a *C*? Listen, I'm lucky I got a *C*. For a while there, I thought I just might be spending my summer vacation sweltering away in summer school.

I don't understand parents at all. They just don't behave rationally most of the time. Now I ask you, if my math is too hard for them to understand, then how can they expect *me* to understand it? Believe me, when I'm a parent, I'm going to be totally reasonable, rational, and sensible all the time. Kind of like you.

You know what? Sometimes I wish I had a younger brother who brought home all *C*s and *D*s. Then I'd look pretty good compared to him and everyone would get off my back and get on his case. Boy, that would be great!

And then again, with my luck, if I did have a younger brother, he'd probably be a genius type and bring home straight *A*s, so maybe I'm better off just sticking with what I've got.

Tell me this, in fifty years how important is this *C* in math really going to be? Right. No one's even going to remember it. So if we're going to forget about it later, why not just forget about it now?

Well, I'd better go. My dad has a new rule for me. I've got to spend an hour on my math every night until I understand it, so I'd better get started. If you never hear from me again, you'll know I'm still working on my math.

Still non-mathematically yours,
Your friend, Leslie

Dear God,

Oh, boy, now we've got another rule. I can't believe anyone can make up so many rules just to make someone else so miserable.

I'm beginning to think teachers and parents get special training somewhere like maybe a POW camp. This time it was Dad again. He says that my brain is rotting away from watching so much television, so he's decided that for every hour of TV I watch, I've got to read a book for an hour.

I still can't believe he's really doing this to me. Do you think he hates me or do you think he just wants to see how miserable he can make me? Except for my positive thinking book, do you know how long it's been since I've read a book which wasn't required reading? Well, neither do I, but it's been a very long time.

You just don't know what it's like having to live with so many rules. There are rules for getting up, rules for going to bed, rules for eating right, rules for what I can do, rules for what I can't do, rules for studying, rules for playing, rules for going out, rules for coming in. I could go on forever, but I think you get the idea. My whole life is just one humongous set of rules.

My parents probably even have my future all planned out for me, but they just haven't bothered to tell me yet.

Oh, oh, that's Mom calling me. She probably has a new rule for me. Just stick around and I'll be right back. I have a feeling I'm going to need someone to talk to.

Well, I'm back and it's definitely bad news. Have you ever taken music lessons? Me either, but it looks like I'm going to.

Between Dad worrying about my brain "rotting away" from watching too much television and Mom on her new culture kick, I don't think I have a chance!

Well, at least she's letting me choose my instrument, so maybe if I pick something really loud like the tuba, they'll pay me to stop practicing after a few weeks.

I know there's probably some weird kid somewhere out there who would give anything to take music lessons, but I'm not that kid. I don't have a musical bone in my entire body and, unless someone gives me a transplant of some kind, I never will have any musical bones.

Well, anyway, what I've got to do now is figure out which instrument I'm going to choose. If you were me, what would you choose?

I've heard the violin is a lot harder than it looks, so I think that's out. How about the guitar? Maybe an electric guitar — that would cost enough, so they just might forget the whole idea of music lessons and things could get back to normal again.

Do you know if you can start right out with an electric guitar or do you have to start out first with an acoustical? Boy, this is really getting complicated, isn't it?

Maybe I should stick with the piano. At least then I wouldn't have to lug it to school every day on the school bus.

Boy, I think this is definitely going to take some time to figure all this out and I don't think you can help me, so I'd better get started figuring,

Non-musically and miserably yours,
Your friend, Leslie

Dear God,

I've got good news and I've got bad news again. Grandma Emerson is coming for Christmas. I suppose you're asking yourself, so what's the "bad news"?

I love my grandmother, but I'm still trying to recover from her visit last summer. I've never been so exhausted in my entire life.

You know how grandmothers used to be people who just sat around in rocking chairs knitting and mending socks all day? Well, I am here to tell you, that is most definitely not true!

I'll tell you what grandmothers are really like. First of all, they have more energy than any kid I've ever known and they just never stop going. They also like to get up early and I *do* mean early because they like to get a lot done before everyone else gets up and gets in their way.

I've got to tell you, I have never been so dog-tired in my entire life. I felt like she was getting me ready for a triathlon.

She had me playing tennis with her every day and don't ask me who always won because I won't tell you. She even wore a tennis dress and tennis socks with little red balls on them which was pretty embarrassing because everyone else on the courts was just wearing shorts and T-shirts.

Actually the tennis wasn't so bad because we usually only played three sets and then it was all over. But the biking was a whole different ball game. She's used to biking all over Sun City where she lives in Arizona and I've got to tell you truthfully there were times when I wasn't sure I was going to make it back home again after some of her "fun" excursions.

And I haven't even told you about the swimming. It seems she belongs to some kind of exercise group in Sun City that keeps track of how far they swim every day because at the end of the year, they get different awards depending on how far they swam. I guess last year she got an award for swimming 300 miles. That's almost a mile a day. Doesn't that just about blow your mind?

Well, at least this year I know what to expect, so I'm going to be prepared. I'm going to get myself in shape even if it kills me.

I wonder if I can get into decent shape in just three days. I think I'm about to find out.

I know this is short, but I'm off to do my push-ups, pull-ups, chin-ups, and anything else that might help me survive her visit.

Non-athletically yours,
Your friend, Leslie

P.S. I sure hope she doesn't know how to ski.

P.P.S. Maybe Mom's vitamins aren't such a bad idea after all.

Dear God,

Well, I made it! Grandma Emerson just left yesterday and I survived her visit. She didn't want to go skiing and we saw a lot of movies while she was here, so it was really fun.

The bad news is that I found out that Mom and Dad are thinking about getting a divorce. I heard them talking to my grandmother about it. Don't you think it's strange that they talked to her about it before they talked to me?

Boy, is this a bummer! Now I'm glad I didn't bug them with my problems. I guess they have enough of their own. I've got to tell you, this has just about flipped me out. Like totally.

You know what this could mean? Weekends, holidays, and vacations with one parent while I live with the other parent. My whole life would be split up into pieces and I'd never know where I'm at or who's who or what's what. Would I have a bedroom both places and where would I keep my electric guitar (if I get one)?

I just don't need this. I have enough problems as it is. All I want is two parents who love each other and love me too. Is that too much to ask?

And what if they end up marrying other people? You know what that would mean? I would have step-brothers and step-sisters and step-mothers and step-fathers all over the place and I'd never know who is who and who is where.

Boy, I sure know one thing. When I get married (*if* I do ever get married), it's going to be forever. What's wrong with adults anyway? Didn't they make a promise to stick it out together no matter what happens? If I make a promise to someone, I keep it. Why can't they?

Why can't they work out their problems the way they're always telling me too? Boy, they call *me* immature and irresponsible!

Divorce is rough on everyone, especially the kids. There were kids at my old school who had to mark their calendars, so they knew who they were staying with when — their mom or their dad. I probably sound kind of down right now, and I guess I am. This is going to take some really heavy thinking and I can use all the help I can get.

It's bad enough that my parents can't get along with each other, but they can't even get along with me. It's like they don't remember what it was like to be young.

Remember how I told you I finally made two new friends at school? Well, how do you keep friends if you can't talk to them? Tell me that.

So anyway I was e-mailing Megan last night and I guess I kind of tied up the phone line, so Dad missed an important business call. Now he's got a new rule that I check with him every night before I use the computer. Around here you can't win for losing! Why don't they just get "call waiting" and then there wouldn't even be any problem?

Maybe my parents just want to make me as miserable as they are and that's why they don't want me to have any friends. Then if I don't have any friends, they know I'll have more time to do slave labor around the house.

You know, when you really think about it, an hour on the computer isn't really all that long. An hour is only 1/24 of the day which leaves a whole 23 hours when I'm *not* on the computer.

Well, anyway, since I can't use the computer for a week, that will give me more time to do some serious thinking and talk to you. How's that for a positive attitude?

Depressingly but positively yours,
Your friend, Leslie

P.S. You know how Ms. Wilson is always telling us that you will never give us more than we can handle? Well, I'm beginning to seriously wonder about that.

Dear God,

I need your frank and honest opinion. Does this kitchen look like a mess to you? Me either. Which just goes to show *again* how unreasonable parents can be.

Okay, so I left a cupboard door open. How do they expect me to get the peanut butter if I don't open the cupboard door?

And there are a few crumbs on the counter. But who counts crumbs? How do I get the bread from way over here to the plate on the counter over there without leaving a few crumbs here and there?

Oh, yeah, and there's a little butter on the refrigerator door, but that's only because I needed milk and I didn't know I was going to have my hands so full by the time I made it to the refrigerator to get the milk.

Okay, so I left the knife drawer open too. Boy, you don't miss anything, do you?

Yeah, yeah, I see the stuff on the stove. That's just spaghetti sauce from last night when I made dinner, so that shouldn't even count for today. Even *they* didn't make any big deal over the spaghetti sauce. After all, it's only on one burner. It's not like it's yucking up the whole stove or anything.

By the way, my ears are fine in spite of all the disaster reports you may have heard from my parents. I am *not* going deaf from playing my music so loud.

It seems that all parents ever do is worry and complain. Why don't they learn to trust us? Life would be so much easier and so much more fun for everyone then.

My parents have got to be the number 1 worriers in the whole world. First, they worry that I am going to go deaf because I play my music so loud. Listen, I can still hear the water faucet dripping before anyone else can and I can even hear the crickets chirping through a closed window. Does that sound like I'm going deaf to you? Not hardly!

Then they worry because they think I listen to my music too much and don't have time to do anything constructive (like read a book). So who's to say what's "constructive" anyway? I do some of my best thinking and get some of my most creative ideas while I'm listening to my music. Does that sound like wasted time to you?

And then they worry that some of my music is "corrupting my morals." Half the time I don't even listen to the words and if the words were really that bad, don't they think I'd know enough to tune them out? By the way, have you ever heard some of *their* music? Talk about real cornball mush — some of it doesn't make any sense at all.

I guess every generation has good music and some not so good, so I think it just comes down to a matter of personal taste in the end. Well, anyway, I'm willing to tolerate their music if they will just be willing to do the same for me. How's that for a mature and tolerant attitude?

I don't know about you, but I am really impressed by my increasing social maturation. All that really means is that I'm more "with it" than I thought I was and I think everything is going to work out okay.

Now that they have definitely decided to get a divorce, I think they're crabbier than ever. I'll tell you one thing. When I get married (*if* I get married) and make a promise to stick by my husband forever, I will really mean it. It will be forever. I think it's very important to keep your promises, don't you?

I know you do because you always keep yours. Hang in there a minute while I change my CD. Oh, oh, Mom's calling me. I'd better go and see what I've done that I shouldn't have done or not done that I should have done.

I know, I know. That wasn't very positive, but I can't be positive all the time.

Musically and creatively yours,
Your friend, Leslie

Dear God,

Things have never been so bad! Mom and Dad finally sat down and talked with me about their divorce. They're calling it a legal separation, but I'm no dummy. Separation, divorce, whatever they call it — it all means the same thing. That our family is breaking up.

You know, I can still remember some of the fun times we used to have. Like all the times we went camping and had to fight off the mosquitoes. And popping popcorn while we watched home movies. And all our trips to the circus and the zoo. And all the weekends at the beach where we roasted hot dogs and marshmallows over the grill.

I wonder what happened. We used to be a real family. We used to have a lot of fun together before everyone started griping about everything everyone else did. Do you think they're getting a divorce because of me? I wonder if Dad is going to get his own apartment just to get away from me. I can't just come right out and ask him if that's why he's moving out, but I still wonder if he's just tired of being a dad. You know, the way some teachers get burned out from teaching, I wonder if some moms and dads can get burned out.

And not only is my family breaking up, but now my body is falling apart on me too. I have finally accepted the fact that I'll always be a flat-chested midget with small eyes and a flat nose, but now I've got a gigantic pimple right on the end of my flat nose.

It's just sitting there as big as life for everyone in the world to see. I've tried covering it with Clearasil and Mom's liquid foundation, but that just makes it look even bigger and blobbier.

I never knew life could be so unfair. Don't you think that there should be some kind of a limit to the number of problems a person has? I'm sure that I've already got more than my share, so why do I have to have any more?

If I were you, I think I would be more careful about who gets stuck with what because it seems to me that some people get an awful lot of the good stuff while some people get stuck with more than their share of the bad stuff.

If what Ms. Wilson says is true about you never giving us more than we can handle, then I think we've really got to have a very serious talk because I am definitely getting overloaded here. Ms. Wilson says that handling problems toughens us up and makes us stronger and that problems can be good for us if we learn how to handle them.

Listen, I don't want to sound like a real wimp or anything, but I think I need a little help here. Are you really giving me all these problems to toughen me up? Maybe you have a lot of confidence in me and think that I can handle them. Not!

I wonder if you realize how discouraged a person can get when she gets stuck with too much of the bad stuff. You probably don't think much about pimples, but pimples can be a really big problem when you're trying to look good and you've got this huge pimple just sitting there on the end of your nose.

You know, I just thought of something. Remember when our life group was talking about why bad things happen and we decided that most of the time you aren't the one who is giving us the problems but that we create a lot of our problems ourselves?

Ms. Wilson told us the important thing to remember is that you will always be there to help us through the tough times when we do have problems.

Okay, now I think I'm beginning to get on the right track again. It certainly isn't your fault that my family is breaking up. And it certainly wasn't your fault that we moved and I had to go to a new school. And you did help me get a friend when I was feeling so lonely. You even got me *two* friends. And you certainly aren't responsible for the pimple on my nose, so I think it's up to me to do something about that myself.

I think I'll go look through the medicine chest again and see what I can find. How do you think a round band-aid look would look? On second thought, that could look even worse than the pimple. Maybe I could color the pimple black with Mom's eyeliner and people would think it's a beauty mark. On second thought, I don't think I've ever seen a beauty mark on the end of someone's nose. I don't want to gross anyone out, I just want to hide what's there.

Say, before I go look through the medicine cabinet, I do have some good news. You remember my math class? Well, I decided to try my new positive thinking approach on that too, so I decided to assume that Mr. Jackson is *not* "out to get me" and is not deliberately trying to confuse me so much that I fail his class.

Now if my first assumption is correct, then I might also assume that he might even want to help me. Right?

Okay, are you still with me so far? So then I decided that if he really wants to help me, I should give him a chance, so I asked to meet with him during my free period. He was free then too, so he told me to come on in.

You are not going to believe this, but he actually seemed *pleased* that I asked for his help. Well, so anyway, I met with him during my free period and I told him just what I've been telling you. How overwhelmed and frustrated I've been feeling because he goes so fast in class that I can't keep up and then I'm never able to understand my homework assignments and so they're always incomplete and usually late.

You know what he's been thinking all this time? He's been thinking that I just didn't care about his class and that I was just another "goof-off" who didn't like school and was just "putting in time" until I could drop out. Boy, how could he ever have thought that?

Well, anyway, he offered to transfer me to a different class which doesn't go quite as fast, but he also told me that he wishes I had talked to him about my problem a lot sooner before I got so far behind.

You know what? I think maybe he's an okay guy after all and you know what else? I wish I had talked to him sooner too. It just goes to show you can't always tell the "bad guys" from the "good guys" right off. I guess you really have to take the time and trouble to get to know someone before you decide.

You know, I think I've learned something from all this. If I have a problem, I shouldn't just stew over it. I should try to do something about it. Like, in this case, talk to Mr. Jackson.

And, speaking of Mr. Jackson, I think I'll go start on my homework for tonight. Even though I'm in a different math class now, I still have him for my teacher. I think that's good because I think I really like Mr. Jackson after all.

I think I'm going to like this new math book too. It explains stuff in a lot more detail and I think I might just end up understanding what I didn't understand before.

Hopefully yours,
Your friend, Leslie

Dear God,

You know this book about positive thinking I've been reading? It says everyone should have a dream. Something you really want and something you really believe in. Then you're supposed to picture it every day in your mind until it becomes an important part of you and, before you know it, your dream will become a reality.

What would your dream be? That we all believe in you and love you the way you love us? I'm not sure what my dream is yet. I guess I'll have to think about that for a while.

So what's new with you? It's pretty much the same old grind around here. Mom's mad at me again because I borrowed her blouse and spilled catsup on it. How did I know we were going to have hamburgers for lunch that day? You can't eat hamburgers without catsup and how did I know the catsup was going to spurt out like that? It's not like I spilled the catsup on her blouse on purpose.

I think she's getting tired of my borrowing her clothes so much, but hers are always cleaner and less wrinkled than mine. Maybe I'll have to try harder to remember to hang her clothes back up after I wear them instead of leaving them on my floor. Then maybe she won't freak out so much when I want to borrow something.

Sometimes I guess I do forget to return some of the things I borrow, but she should realize that I've got a lot on my mind these days and I can't be expected to remember everything.

She keeps telling me that I should treat her clothes the same way I would want my clothes to be treated. Well, I do. I don't hang up my clothes either.

It seems to me that life is simply a matter of deciding on your priorities — deciding which things are important and which things aren't so important. Then you don't waste your time doing the things that aren't important, so that you have time to do the important things. Did you get all that? I think I'm beginning to figure out a lot of these things for myself, thanks to that book. You just have to have a really well-organized mind like mine and then it's easy to sort all this stuff out.

Actually, I think it's more than just the catsup and my borrowing her clothes that's got Mom so uptight. Now that Dad's got his own apartment, she seems even moodier and pickier than she was before.

By the way, how often do you think I should shampoo my hair? I only shampoo it once a day and I know some kids who shampoo their hair every morning and every night.

Well, now Mom's complaining that I use up all the hot water and there's none left for her. I know that's not true because I listen to a CD while I'm in the shower and I'm always out of the shower before the CD even finishes.

Now you just know that one CD is not going to use up all the hot water, right?

You know what I think? I think mothers must just like to nag because they sure do enough of it. But the more she nags, the more I tune her out, so I don't even hear her nagging most of the time. Isn't that smart? I wonder if all kids learn to do that as part of their survival plan.

I'll show you what I mean about her nagging. She just doesn't nag about the hot water. She even complains because I use too many bath towels when I shower. All I use is one for me, one for my hair, and one to stand on when the bath mat gets left inside the shower and gets so wet I can't use it.

She claims there are never any dry towels left for her. Well, all she has to do is put more towels in the bathroom and then there'll be plenty of towels for both of us. Now why couldn't she have figured that out for herself? Sometimes I really wonder about mothers.

I've already told you how she nags me about my music, but it's got to be loud or I won't be able to hear it while I'm in the shower. And you can't take a shower without music.

That would be like eating cereal without bananas or strawberries on it. You just wouldn't do that. I keep explaining this to her, but she just doesn't seem to get it.

I bet I know what's coming next. More rules! I bet now there'll be rules about the number of towels I can use, the length of time I can spend in the shower, the number of times I can shampoo my hair a week, and so on and so on and so on.

I can hear her calling me, so I've got to go.

Imaginatively yours,
Your friend, Leslie

P.S. Do you think she might ban my CD player from the bathroom? That would really be a low blow!

Dear God,

In our life group we've been talking a lot about prayer. I always thought praying was pretty easy. I used to think that I just had to ask you for what I wanted and that was all there was to it. But I guess there's a lot more to it than that.

I've been learning that it's important to pray a lot. Somewhere in the Bible it says, "Pray without ceasing." I don't think I'd get much done if I did that, but I guess what it means is that we should be thinking about you a lot even when we're not actually praying.

Like before we do something, we should just kind of mentally check it out with you to see if it's okay with you. Or when we're wondering about something or have to make a decision about something, we should just kind of ask ourselves what we think you would want us to do in that situation.

I think I can do that. Actually, I think that's what I've been doing these last few months. And it does make life a lot easier, knowing you're always there to help me.

Ms. Wilson says that the more we pray or talk to you, the easier it will be for us to know what you want us to do. That makes sense to me. Like I know what my mom and dad want me to do in most situations (even if I don't always do it), so I guess it's pretty much the same way with you. I'll kind of know inside myself if it's something you approve of or not.

Okay, I can dig all that, but there's even more I didn't know. I didn't know that it's important to thank you and praise you a lot. I think a lot of times I forget to thank you for stuff because I'm always so busy asking you to help me with new stuff.

From now on, I'm going to thank you a lot more. I'm sure you like to feel appreciated the same way the rest of us like to feel appreciated.

Like when Mom slips up and thanks me for making dinner or when Dad used to thank me for shoveling the driveway, that always made me feel really good. I think everyone likes to feel appreciated, so I'm definitely going to try to remember to thank you a lot more in the future.

We've also been learning about intercessory prayer. That just means praying for other people. I guess it's okay to ask for things for ourselves the way I've been doing, but it's also important to pray for other people too. Especially for people who are sick or who have problems. Like those two boys in my class who were using drugs. Do you remember how I asked you to help them? I guess that was intercessory prayer and I didn't even know it at the time.

And I guess it's important to pray for our country and even for people we don't really know. Like the people who run our government and our schools. I already pray for my family, but I guess I should be praying for lots of other people too.

I also learned that confession is part of prayer. That just means that we should talk to you about our mistakes and ask for your forgiveness. No sweat, I can do that. It'll be a lot easier telling you when I mess up than telling Mom or Dad. Actually, I kind of like that part. It gives me someone to kind of talk things over with when I don't want to talk to Mom or Dad.

And I also learned that I'm not supposed to do all the talking all the time. I guess we're also supposed to be doing some listening. No one ever told me that before, so all this time I guess I've been doing all the talking.

The way Ms. Wilson explains it is that we're supposed to be quiet some of the time so that you can talk to our heart. If we're always talking, we don't give you a chance to really tell us what *you* want.

Is that why we have two ears and just one mouth? Because you want us to listen more? I will most definitely give that some very serious thought.

I think I'll begin practicing some of this stuff by thanking you for Ariel. She's the goldfish I got at the school fair last night. A goldfish isn't exactly my idea of a "pet," but Jasmine, Megan, and I were at the fair and there was this tiny little goldfish in a plastic bag all by herself, so Jasmine loaned me a dollar so I could buy Ariel and bring her home.

I just knew Jasmine and Megan would like each other and they do. The three of us are going to the mall this morning to buy Ariel a regular fish bowl with some colored rocks and maybe even a little shell of some kind, so she doesn't have to stay in the pickle jar.

My problem — or I guess I should say Ariel's problem — is that I think she needs a friend. I don't want her to be lonely the way I was, so I want to get another goldfish today while we're at the pet store.

My question is, do I just bring home another goldfish without warning Mom or should I check it out with her first to be sure it's okay?

Right now she's at the beauty salon getting her hair frosted, so I think maybe that's the answer. If I go to the mall now, I can just leave her a note telling her I'll be bringing another goldfish home.

That way she won't have a chance to say no and I'll have done the responsible thing by telling her what I'm doing before I actually do it.

I think I'll walk over to Megan's right now before Mom gets back. Did I tell you that Jasmine lives just a block away from the mall, so Megan and I will stop by for her on the way to the mall? See ya later.

Craftily yours,
Your friend, Leslie

P.S. You want to know something interesting? Mom never got her hair frosted when Dad was still living with us. What do you suppose that means?

P.P.S. In case you're wondering about those white rats, Mom said she would "think about it." At least she hasn't said, "No," but by the time she finishes "thinking about it," Munch and Scrunch will probably be "senior citizens." Don't you think those are great names? I decided to name them, even though they're still stuck in the lab, because I think it's important for them to know that someone cares enough about them to give them names. Right?

Dear God,

Do you think I'm too young to date? You know, go out with someone of the opposite sex and have a lot of fun.

No one's really asked me out yet, but I just thought I'd be ready in case anyone does.

Both Mom and Dad think thirteen is too young to go out on a real date alone with a boy, but they agreed that I could go roller-skating or bowling or to a movie if a whole group goes.

Sometimes I think my parents are still back in the Dark Ages. I don't think they even know that some of the girls in my class already have steady boyfriends. In fact, they'd probably die right on the spot if they knew some of the things that some of the girls in my class are already doing.

Did you know that I can't even wear any blush or lipstick yet except on special occasions? Some of the girls in my class are already wearing blush, lipstick, eyeliner, mascara, eye shadow, foundation — the whole works. And they even get to wear it to school every day.

And you know how I can only wear pink fingernail polish? You should see some of the colors the other girls wear. There are reds, purples, browns, blacks, and even silver and gold — just about any color you can imagine and then some. One girl even wears sparkles on her fingernails and on her eyelids. How do you suppose she gets them on? With glue? And, more important, how do you think she gets them off?

I'm not really into sparkles myself, but I do think I'm ready for a more mature nail polish color. Nobody who's anybody at our school wears pink.

How do you suppose I can get my parents to realize that I'm not as young as they think I am? A younger brother or sister might come in handy at a time like this because I'd probably seem a lot older then and they'd let me do more things.

On the other hand, I might get stuck having to babysit all the time, so scratch that idea. Besides, if Mom and Dad are getting a divorce, it's not likely I'm going to get a brother or sister anyway.

I think this is another of those problems that's going to take some very heavy thinking.

Talk to ya later.

Anachronistically yours,
Your friend, Leslie

P.S. I learned that word in my science class. It means something that's outmoded or out-of-date.

Dear God,

Megan just called to tell me that a boy from our school died this morning from meningitis. His name was Erik and he was on our school tennis team.

I guess he hadn't been feeling too well for several days, but he didn't want to miss the hockey playoffs, so he went to the hockey game last night even though he wasn't feeling all that great.

Then sometime late last night he got a lot worse and his parents took him to the hospital and he died this morning. Just like that, he's gone.

I didn't know him very well or anything, but his locker was just across from mine and I saw him just about every day.

You know, last year at my old school a kid came down with meningitis, but he was only out of school a little over a week and in less than a month, he was playing basketball and everything again.

It makes me wonder why some people die and some people don't. Here we have two kids with meningitis and one kid makes it and one kid doesn't. Why?

I'm going to have to ask Ms. Wilson what she thinks about this because I sure don't have any answers myself.

You know, I'm really glad now that I didn't drop out of my life group. You can ask questions like this there and you don't feel dumb. No one laughs at you and I'm beginning to feel pretty safe there.

Contemplatively yours,
Your friend, Leslie

P.S. Sometime I'll have to talk to you about Grandma Morgan because I still don't understand why she had to die when she did. Don't get me wrong, I love my Grandma Emerson a lot, but that doesn't mean I don't still miss Grandma Morgan.

Dear God,

I just got home from my life group and I've got a lot to tell you.

During our small group session, I asked Ms. Wilson what I told you I was going to ask her. You know, why some people die and some people don't die when they have basically the same problem.

Guess what? She didn't have any answers either, but it got our group to thinking and we spent the whole session just talking about this.

Crystal thought maybe it depended on how much you pray. Like maybe one kid prayed a lot and maybe one kid didn't. We talked about that for a while, but then we decided we didn't believe that was the answer.

We talked about some of the missionaries who have died or been killed and if anyone prays a lot, those people certainly do, but they still get sick and die sometimes. And my minister in my old neighborhood died of colon cancer and I know he prayed a lot. So I'm pretty sure that's not the answer.

Elizabeth thought maybe it had something to do with how good you are. You know, like if you're really nice to everyone and do everything you're supposed to do, then maybe you get to live. We talked about that for a long time too, but we decided that wasn't the answer either.

We all knew really special people who are always doing things for other people, but sometimes they die or have really bad things happen to them. So we decided that it wasn't as simple as the good guys live and the bad guys don't.

What we *did* decide is that bad things are going to happen to everyone and that you never promised that bad things wouldn't happen to us. What you did promise was that you would always be there for us and never leave us, so that we could use some of your strength to get us through the bad times when we didn't feel we had enough strength of our own.

It seems to me that the bottom line here is that there are just some questions we won't have the answers to until we get to heaven and can ask you about them. So I guess it means that we're just going to have to live our lives by faith, believing that things will always work out in the end.

Somewhere in the Bible it says something about everything working for good for those who love you and believe, so I think maybe we just have to accept that on faith.

We talked a lot about the definition of "faith," and I guess it means believing in things we can't really see with our eyes. In this case, it means believing that you will always be there for us whenever we need you.

You promised that you would answer whenever we called and I know that you keep all your promises. I think I see it as kind of living by the spirit and the heart more than by our physical senses.

It's kind of like believing that the flowers are going to bloom again in the spring even though we don't see any physical evidence of that with our eyes when everything is covered with snow.

Or believing that the ducks and geese are going to return in the spring even though we don't see a single goose or duck all winter. When you think about it, I think we accept a lot of things on faith.

So I think what it all comes down to is that I'm simply not going to get all the answers to all my questions. I think that believing when we don't have all the answers and when we don't always understand is what faith is all about.

In a way, it seems that it's kind of testing our faith this way. Just think about it for a minute. If we could understand everything and had all the answers, we wouldn't really need much faith to believe, but this way we have to learn to trust you and believe *because* we don't have all the answers.

I think I can live with that, but I think I might also just begin to keep a list of all the things I don't understand, so that I can talk to you about them when I see you.

Boy, I am really zonked out, so I'm going to hit the sack. Have you ever noticed how exhausting really serious thinking can be?

I hope I don't have trouble getting to sleep. Sometimes when I'm thinking this hard, it's hard to shut my brain down and unwind. Well, here goes!

Thoughtfully but exhaustedly yours,
Your friend, Leslie

Dear God,

Do you know what Tom said today? You know, the boy in my math class with the locker next to mine. Well, I finally found out his name from Megan's friend Sarah who knows a friend of Tom's.

Well, anyway, Tom told me he likes my eyes because they're so dark and deep set. I'm not sure what he means by "deep set," but I think it must be okay, don't you? He didn't even mention *small*. You know, maybe he's not as shy as I thought. In a million years I would never have said anything to him about his eyes. Not that I haven't noticed them because I have. They're kind of a greenish-blue.

He hasn't asked me to go roller-skating or anything yet, but telling me that he likes my eyes is sure a good start, don't you think? With my new positive approach to life, I'll probably have him totally bonkers over me before he even knows what hit him.

I thought of asking you to help me out here, but I decided that would be taking unfair advantage. Well, I think I'd better get busy planning my next move. Maybe I'll set up a list of daily goals for myself, kind of like I was devising the strategy for a military campaign.

Speaking of goals, you know what I've noticed? You know how I've been setting all those goals for myself ever since I read that book on positive thinking?

Like when I decided to try to make one new friend? And now I have two friends. And like last week when I decided to surprise Mom and I gave my room a complete overhaul? Remember how I got so carried away that I even cleaned under my bed by mistake?

Well, anyway, what I've noticed is that working to achieve my goal is sometimes more fun than actually achieving my goal. What I guess I mean is that I like achieving the goals I set for myself because it gives me a feeling of accomplishment, but then there's also a little feeling of letdown at the same time. It's like then I've got this little empty space inside me which needs filling up again. Why do you think that is? Does that ever happen to you?

Did that happen to you after you created the earth and the people and animals and everything? Did you want to set another goal and do something more?

Maybe not, since you rested after you finished making everything. Well, anyway, since I was feeling a little down, I set another goal for myself and now I feel okay again. Does this make any sense to you? I'm not sure I understand it, so I was hoping you would.

What if someone achieved all his goals? Do you think then he would feel more bad or more good? I really wonder about that. It almost seems to me that a person always has to be in the process of trying to achieve some kind of goal in order to be really happy. What do you think?

It's kind of like when I'm weeding the gardens. I complain a lot while I'm doing it, but then the yard looks so great after I'm done that I find myself looking around to see if there's anything else I can do to make the yard look even better. Or like when you paint one room, and then the other rooms seem to look worse somehow, and so you figure maybe you'd better paint them too.

I think I'll have to give this some more thought because it's still pretty confusing to me. And I still don't understand why I cleaned under my bed. No one else ever even looks under there.

Well, I'm going to go start plotting my strategy for Tom.

Militarily yours,
Your friend, Leslie

P.S. Maybe Mom was right after all. Maybe small eyes *can* be beautiful.

Dear God,
You'll never believe this. I swear things are going from bad to worse. Yeah, yeah, I know what you're thinking. Well, I can't have a positive attitude *all* the time, can I?

Now my mom wants to get a job. Since it's April Fool's Day today, at first I thought she was kidding, but she wasn't. She was dead serious.

So what's wrong with just being a wife and mother? Well, maybe she won't be a wife much longer, but what's wrong with just being a mother?

I can tell you right now what's going to happen if she gets a job. It will be TV dinners and pizza delivery. I like pizza, but not every day for the rest of my life.

Mom says now that I'm older, she doesn't have enough to do to keep busy and that if they do get a divorce, then they'll need the extra money, so it sounds like I don't really have much choice about the whole matter.

Well, who knows? Maybe I'm worrying too soon. Maybe Mom won't even be able to find a job. After all, what could she do? She's only been a mom all her adult life, so she probably doesn't know how to do much of anything and I've heard that jobs are really hard to get these days. I guess I'll just have to wait and see what happens.

Maybe this would be a good time to ask Mom about the white rats again. Don't you think she's had enough time to think about them by now?

It's getting so that I don't even like going to the science lab anymore. There they are waiting for me to take them home and all I can tell them is that my mom is "still thinking about it." Wouldn't you think they would start feeling kind of rejected if they think no one wants them? I know I would.

Maybe I should give my positive thinking a try again. After all, what do I have to lose? Or maybe I should leave the book around where Mom can see it. I think she could use a massive dose of some positive thinking right about now.

70

Oh, oh, Mom's calling me, so I've got to go. I'll get back to you as soon as I can. I wonder what I've done now.

Fearfully yours,
Your friend, Leslie

P.S. I just want you to know how glad I am that I have you to help me through all this. I wonder if Mom knows how much you could help her too. Has she been talking to you much?

Dear God,

Boy, now I think I know what the expression "blood, sweat, and tears" means. I think I just lost some of each. You should have been there, you never would have believed all the commotion.

I finally won, but I'm not sure it was worth it. For the last month I've been asking Mom for her permission to get my ears pierced, but she wanted to see how Dad felt about it, so she just told me she would "think about it." Boy, that seems to be her line for everything these days, doesn't it?

Well, anyway, when Dad stopped by today to see how everything was going, she told him about my wanting to get my ears pierced. The way they carried on, you'd think I was going to lose all my blood or go off to active duty somewhere on the front lines.

Good grief, pierced ears are no big deal. Everyone has pierced ears these days. I know babies who have pierced ears. I even know boys who have a pierced ear. That just goes to show that it's no big deal if even babies are getting their ears pierced.

Did you know that some girls have two or three holes in each ear? I should have told Mom and Dad that. Then maybe one hole in each ear would have sounded pretty tame to them.

There are even kids at school who have pierced noses and navels. I kid you not, some kids at this school are wearing rings through their noses and I've heard via the grapevine that there are kids who have rings through parts of their bodies that I won't even mention.

Mom and Dad wanted me to wait till I was sixteen before I "mutilated my body," but what's so special about being sixteen? I want pierced ears now and I'll still want them when I'm sixteen, so why wait?

You know, I know for a fact that my mom had pierced ears when she was six because Grandma Emerson told me. So why all this fuss about something so simple? I think this divorce thing is really getting to them. I sure hope they don't come totally unglued or anything.

Well, anyway, I won the first round. They finally agreed that I could get my ears pierced as long as I have it done by a professional and not by one of my friends. That seemed fair enough, so I agreed to that and now I'm getting ready for the second round.

The second round will be about what kinds of earrings I can wear.

I won't start right out with the big hoops and the long dangles. I'll have to use a little psychology on them. That just means getting someone to do something they really don't want to do but which you want them to do and they end up doing it because they don't realize they're really doing something they don't want to do.

Did you get all that? In this case, it means starting out with the earrings *they* like and ending up with the earrings *I* like without their ever knowing what happened. I hope!

By the way, I think I'm finally making some headway as far as improving our parent-child communication (I learned about this in one of Mom's women's magazines). Parent-child communication is very important because parents can become very depressed and feel like failures as parents if they don't feel their kids can really talk to them.

Well, anyway, you know how my book on positive thinking says to "keep your cool" and to think positively even when the other guy doesn't? Well, I did and they didn't and it worked because when I did, then eventually they did too and everything turned out okay in the end. You know, maybe the guy who wrote that book isn't such a weirdo after all. Maybe he really *does* know what he's talking about.

Well, I've got to go. Now that I've got them in a good mood, I want to try to keep them that way for a while. I think I'll go offer to make dinner. That will really blow their minds!

Talk to ya later.

Psychologically yours,
Your friend, Leslie

P.S. Don't you think it's great that I'm learning so much? Did I tell you that I even like reading books now? Books are actually pretty cool. You can learn a lot from them and have a lot of fun at the same time. When I'm reading a book, it's like I'm in a whole different world and I can just forget all the problems I have in this world.

P.P.S. Did I ever tell you about the kids at school with the orange hair? I don't think that's really my bag, but it's certainly something to think about, isn't it?

Dear God,

You will not believe this! In fact, I'm not sure I believe it. Did you hear all that screaming just now? Well, that was Mom screaming at me because I didn't fold the bathroom towels the right way.

Now I ask you, who really cares if bathroom towels are folded in half or in thirds? Do you care? Me either. At least they're folded. See what I mean about my not being appreciated for the stuff I do do and how Mom is always on my back for the stuff I don't do?

Would you even notice how the towels were folded? Of course not. You have better things to do with your time and so do I.

Mothers can be so unreasonable. Sometime we've got to have a heart-to-heart talk about mothers because I have a few suggestions for you.

In the future, could you try to make them a little less critical and a little more mellow? When Mom is mellow, she is really one super mom, but most of the time she's rushing around, trying to do twenty things at once.

You know what I miss the most? No more family dinners. We used to have some really great talks during dinner, but that was before everyone got so busy and so irritable. I guess those days are gone forever.

Believe me, if and when I become a mother, I am definitely going to be mellow and I sure won't get bent all out of shape just because someone folds the towels the wrong way. Besides, who's to say that *her* way is the right way anyway?

You know, I'm beginning to think maybe Mom is right. Maybe she doesn't have enough to do. If she had a job, I'm sure she'd be worrying about something more important than bathroom towels. Do you think she might be easier to live with then?

You know, when Mom and Dad first started talking about getting a divorce, I was so overwhelmed by the whole idea that I thought I'd self-destruct. But then things weren't so great when they were still living together either.

They were both always so stressed out and uptight that I just knew one or both of them were going to yell at me as soon as I stepped through the door.

It got to the point where I didn't even want to bring Megan or Jasmine home with me because it was like walking through a mine field. I never knew what to do to avoid setting off a big explosion.

At least with Dad in his own apartment, I only have to worry about Mom. Sometimes she's really crabby like today about the towels, but there's other days when she seems a lot more relaxed and not so irritable.

She's still pretty moody, but I can live with that. I figure it'll take a while for her to really adjust to being a single parent after living so many years as a family.

Do you smell that? It smells like chocolate chip cookies baking. Mom hasn't baked chocolate chip cookies for over a year.

Do you think she's doing it to make up for yelling at me over the towels? Or do you think she's doing it because she's happier and less uptight now that Dad's left? I don't think I can come right out and ask her something like that, do you?

Well, thanks for listening. I think I'll go check on the chocolate chip cookies.

Hungrily yours,
Your friend, Leslie

Dear God,

Have you seen my hips? What I don't understand is how I can be so short, how my legs can be so skinny, and how my hips can still be so big! I imagine you probably get a lot of complaints about big hips.

Dad's coming over tonight to celebrate my birthday and we're going to go somewhere really nice to eat. That means there'll be millions of people and they'll all be staring at my hips. Well, maybe not millions. Would you believe thousands? Okay, okay, I'll settle for a hundred. But, anyway, they're all going to be staring at my hips, wondering why I don't do something about them (my hips, that is).

My favorite long blouse which covers my hips is in the dirty clothes hamper and Mom won't let me take it out of the hamper so I can wear it. Believe me, no one at the restaurant is going to know that I took the blouse out of the hamper, so why can't I wear it? I bet if it were up to you, you'd let me wear it. You *would*, wouldn't you?

Maybe she'll let me borrow one of her blouses. On second thought, I don't think I'd better ask her since she wasn't able to get the catsup stain out of the last blouse I borrowed from her.

By the way, that catsup stain was definitely not my fault. There was absolutely no way I could know that the catsup was going to spurt out at me the way it did with no warning at all.

Besides, how was I supposed to know that you had to wash catsup stains out right away? No one ever told me, so how would I know? At least I put it in the dirty clothes hamper and not under my bed. She should at least give me some credit for that.

But what do I do about tonight? I can't go to some fancy restaurant if I can't find something which will cover my hips.

Well, I've got to go. This is a real emergency.

Critically yours,
Your friend, Leslie

P.S. I know what you're thinking. That I was going to be satisfied with the way I looked and not complain any more about any of my body parts. You're right as usual. Looking at the big picture, my hips are most definitely not up there at the top of my list of concerns.

P.P.S. I'm trying, I really am, but it's not always easy to keep focused on that bigger picture. I bet you have this problem with a lot of your children, don't you? You must be a really, really patient dad. I hope that when I'm a mom, I'll be as patient with my kids as you are with yours.

P.P.P.S. Now that I'm getting so much figured out, I think I will most definitely want to be a mom some day. After I get through school and everything, of course.

Dear God,

I'm back from dinner and everything went great. Mom and Dad didn't snipe at each other all night and I got some really super computer software for my birthday. Now I can set up my own computer print shop and make all my own cards and lots of other stuff.

I also got a great new fantasy book called *Growing Wings* which looks really cool. The best part about the book is what my mom wrote inside. "To Leslie — may you grow your own wings and soar as high as your dreams will take you."

It still seems kind of weird to me how for so many years I never read a book I didn't have to and now I can't stop reading. I read in bed every night before I go to sleep and it's kind of like my own magic time. It's just me and the book and I don't worry about anything else.

Well, anyway, when we got home, Dad left right away and Mom and I went out to the kitchen and snacked on chocolate chip cookies and milk.

We had a really great talk and you know what? She told me lots of stuff I never even knew.

Did you know that she's lonely a lot of the time? You probably already knew that, but I didn't. I guess I just assumed that moms are always so busy doing housework and driving their kids around to all their activities that they wouldn't have time to be lonely.

She told me that most of her friends are working now and that they don't seem to have much time to call her anymore. And even when she does see them, they're always talking about their jobs and she never feels she has much to say to them.

You know what? I guess I've always just thought of parents as parents but never as real people just like us. All this time I've been so busy worrying about my own problems that I've never really stopped to think about all the problems that parents have.

I guess moving to a new neighborhood and a new house was just as hard on Mom as it was on me. Does she talk to you about her problems the way I do?

I think maybe I've been spending too much time feeling sorry for myself when maybe I should be spending a little more time looking at what's going on around me.

Would you mind terribly if I spent a little less time with you and a little more time with Mom for a while? I think she really needs someone to talk to right now.

Thanks, I knew you'd understand. You know, Ms. Wilson is always talking about the importance of having "an attitude of gratitude" and I think I'm beginning to understand what she means by that.

I think maybe I'll make a list of all the things I'm grateful for and you'll be right up there at the top of my list. I think if I spend more of my time focusing on the good stuff and less time focusing on the bad stuff, I'll feel a lot better, don't you?

Maturely yours,
Your friend, Leslie

P.S. Maybe I'll even try talking to Dad sometime. You know, *really* talking.

Monday, May 6

Dear God,

I think I'm really beginning to get the hang of this positive thinking stuff. You know how I never liked to go places where there would be lots of people because I didn't want people staring at my hips?

Well, now I know that everyone in the world is not going to be staring at my hips. My positive thinking book says to "lighten up" and not take life or yourself too seriously. It says that no one is perfect and that if you spend all your time and energy worrying about all the things that are wrong with you, it won't leave you much time to have fun and enjoy life.

I think this kind of fits in with what Ms. Wilson was saying about you making each one of us beautiful in our own way. I kind of like thinking of myself as a special creation put together just the way you wanted me to be.

Did I ever tell you about Kelly? She's one of the girls in my life group and she's been telling us about her cousin who's anorexic. I guess her cousin got down to 62 pounds because she just never ate and she didn't eat because she thought she was "too fat."

Kelly said that she and her cousin would look in the same mirror at the same time, but they both saw very different things. Her cousin saw herself as "fat" while Kelly saw her cousin as so skinny that she looked like she had just come out of a POW camp. Kelly said that when her cousin wore a bikini, she looked like those skeletons that are hanging in the science lab at school.

Her cousin's in treatment now, but I guess it's going to take a long time for her to begin to see herself as she really is. It's funny what the mind can do, isn't it? It just goes to show how important our thinking is and how important it is to put the right thoughts into our mind.

If Kelly's cousin had been in a group like ours a long time ago, she might never have developed her eating disorder because she would have seen herself as special just the way she was. Maybe when she finishes treatment, she can join a group like ours.

81

I don't even know Kelly's cousin, but I think she's helped me to start being a lot more grateful for what I have and not to complain so much about what I don't have. Maybe I'll even start with my teeth. My teeth really do look great and I can smile now without being embarrassed.

I think that book is really right about "lightening up" and not taking yourself so seriously. You remember how serious I was the first few months of school and how everything seemed of earth-shaking importance to me? Well, I've got to tell you, those first few months really weren't much fun and I was beginning to get pretty down on myself.

But then a few things started going right for me and I began to feel that maybe the whole world wasn't against me after all.

And then I began to realize that most of the other kids were okay too and even those kids who weren't so nice to me were probably unhappy themselves.

I think you usually feel better if you're nice to other people because it makes you feel better about yourself and so when you run into someone who is deliberately mean and rotten (I don't really think there are very many people like that), you can bet they're really unhappy themselves. It took me a long time to figure that out, but now that I have, I think maybe I can be nicer to those people who aren't always so nice to me.

I think I've come a long way this year, don't you? I think I can even laugh at some of my problems now. Like my big hips and my flat nose.

In one of our life groups Ms. Wilson told us about her youth minister who read them a story about a man who was so unhappy because he had no shoes until he met a man who had no feet.

That really made me think. No matter what your problem is, it seems there's always someone with an even bigger problem than yours. Sometimes a lot bigger. I think that story will help me keep things in proper perspective, so I don't worry so much about those things which really aren't all that important anyway.

I know you don't do any dumb things, but I still do a lot of dumb things and I'm trying not to get all bent out of shape anymore, either feeling sorry for myself or being mad at myself.

I figure I do some pretty smart things too and my mistakes are all just part of living and learning.

You know, life really isn't all that hard once you figure some of these things out. Maybe I'll even write a book explaining some of this stuff to other kids, so they won't have to spend so much time having to figure everything out for themselves.

Well, I've gotta go.

Winningly yours,
Your friend, Leslie

Dear God,

Good news! I think I've got a dream now. You know how my positive thinking book said everyone should have a dream? Well, I think I've got one now.

I'm going to be a writer and write books for kids. Remember how I told you I was really beginning to like my English class? Well, today we got our essays back and I got an A- on mine and that's without even really trying. Just think what I could do if I really tried! Ms. Evans even wrote a note at the end of my essay telling me that I write well and to "keep up the good work." How about that!

You know, English is very important if you're going to be a writer, so it looks like I'm already off to a good start.

I've also heard that a good writer writes about something he knows a lot about. Well, I know a lot about being a kid. I was a kid for a long time before I grew up, so I've got plenty of firsthand experience.

If I can just remember what it was like being a kid after I'm not a kid anymore, I'll have it made. Do you think I'll still be able to think like a kid even when I'm really old like Mom?

That book says that just *believing* you can do something is half the battle, so since I already believe I can be a good writer some day, I figure I'm already halfway there.

I guess I'd better go now because I've got a lot of writing to do. Maybe I forgot to tell you, but the other half of the battle is lots of *hard work*, so if I'm going to be a famous writer, I'd better start practicing now. The sooner I start, the sooner I'll be a famous author and the sooner I'll be able to start making up some rules of my own.

Bye for now.

Famously yours,
Your friend, Leslie

Dear God,

It just occurred to me that I can practice my writing on you, so I'm back.

Did I tell you that I have three friends now and they're coming over tonight to pop popcorn and watch TV? Boy, who would have ever thought I'd end up with three friends the way things started out? It just goes to show that if I hang in there and bite the bullet while I'm waiting for you to help me, things will always work out okay.

Poor Mom, she's really feeling down lately. All her adult life she's been either a wife or a mother or both and now she's feeling that she might not be either one much longer seeing as how Dad has already moved out and I'm growing up so fast.

I don't think she's really sure just what she is at this point. That magazine of hers I was reading the other day calls this an "identity crisis." I think an identity crisis is what happens when you no longer feel needed by anyone and you begin to wonder what you're good for. (Kind of the way Munch and Scrunch must feel by now.)

It's what my positive thinking book has been saying all along. That if you don't feel good about yourself, then you can begin having all sorts of problems.

You know what I think? I think Mom *does* need a job. There must be something she could do. Maybe I can read over the want ads with her and give her some encouragement. I think she needs a dream too, but I think I'll just concentrate on the job first.

It must be really tough not to feel very good about yourself. Hey, did you hear what I just said? Boy, have I come a long way! I'd almost forgotten that it wasn't too long ago that I wasn't feeling too terrific myself. Boy, that just goes to show what a positive attitude can do.

I think maybe I should add Mom to my prayer list too. I know I always ask you to take care of her and Dad, but I haven't really asked you to help her find a job. And after all, if there's anyone who can help her with this problem, you can.

85

I guess this is what Ms. Wilson calls "intercessory prayer." I'm asking you to help someone else. I think you like it when we pray for other people, so I'm going to try to remember to do it a lot more.

Speaking of prayer, you know what Pastor Hardy said last Sunday? He told us that if we have a problem, all we have to do is take it to you and you'll always help us.

I wish someone had told me that a long time ago. Do you realize how much time and energy I've wasted all these years trying to work out all my problems all by myself? If it hadn't been for Ms. Wilson and our life group, I'd probably still be trying to do everything all by myself.

He also told us that you really like helping us with our problems because it gives us the opportunity to deepen our relationship with you and gives us the chance to get to know each other better. I guess it's the same as with any relationship, the more you share with someone, the closer you get to that person and the more you begin to trust that person.

It just goes to show that if you know some of the ground rules, life isn't all that hard. I really do think I should write that book for kids now that I'm learning so much. I think I have a lot I could share with them which might help them.

Remember how in the beginning I was wondering if prayer really works and then we decided in our life group that you definitely listen to our prayers and you definitely answer them, even though sometimes you may not answer them in the way we expect you to?

Well, Pastor Hardy told us pretty much the same thing. He was quoting Matthew and Luke and he asked us if a parent who loves his child would give him a stone when that child asks for bread? Or would he give his child a serpent when he asks for a fish? Of course not.

Then we know for sure that since you're the most loving parent of all, that you are going to give your children good gifts and not gifts that would hurt us. I think that makes a lot of sense and I especially liked that part about the bread and the stone.

Would you ever give your child a stone when he asked for bread? Of course not. I think we're back to that larger picture again and, of course, faith. We have to learn to trust you to do what's best for us even when we may not see that larger picture yet ourselves.

Do you think Pastor Hardy has been telling us this stuff all the time and I just wasn't listening? I really don't know, but I think I'm going to listen more from now on, so that I don't miss any more important stuff.

Well, I've got to go. I promised Mom I would cook dinner tonight, so that she can have some extra time to herself. You should have seen her face. I think she thought I had flipped out for sure. Then she got this huge smile on her face and she gave me a giant hug. Boy, it sure feels great when someone you love is happy. It makes life a lot more fun for everyone, doesn't it?

I think I'll make spaghetti. Spaghetti is really fun to make because you can pretty much just "ad lib" as you go. You know, add a little of this and a little of that. You can be as creative as you want to because that's what spaghetti's all about. Kind of like life, right? Yeah, yeah, I won't forget to clean the stove afterward.

Joyfully yours,
Your friend, Leslie

Dear God,

Good news! I can bring Munch and Scrunch home. At least for the summer. Mom says we'll see how it goes during the summer and then she'll decide whether or not they can stay permanently. I think that's fair enough, don't you?

How would you like to be waiting all this time for a good home? They must be feeling pretty rejected by now. I hope this experience doesn't permanently damage their personalities.

Just in case Mom didn't agree to let me bring Munch and Scrunch home, I had a backup plan all ready. Charlie's a kid in my homeroom who's already got four dogs, two cats, three ferrets, and a snake at his house, so I don't think his mom would even notice the white rats if he took them home. He told me one time that she never even goes in his room because she's afraid of what she might find there.

I don't know if I've told you about Charlie. He's the kid who's always late to school, but he makes up such really terrific excuses that you just have to admire his creativity. Anyway, I think that Charlie would have taken the guys home if I hadn't.

More good news! I think my nose is a little less flat. I'm not sure myself if it is really less flat or if it just looks less flat to me because I'm feeling better about myself now. But who cares? Listen, whatever works is okay with me. I don't have to understand all the old nitty-gritty of everything.

I know for a fact that I am definitely taller. I have grown half an inch over the last year because I just had my physical and the nurse measured me. Isn't that really super?

You know what I think did it? My new positive attitude. I think having a positive attitude is really important for just about everything in life, don't you?

If you just know good things are going to happen to you and you visualize them happening in your mind, then good things will probably happen. I think my new philosophy of life is going to be, "Go for it!"

I'm really beginning to feel on top of things for the first time in my entire life and it's a good feeling. I'm beginning to realize that all of us (even parents) have problems or "challenges" and that a lot of our problems are pretty much the same for everyone.

I think a lot of those problems are really all about how we feel about ourselves because that determines how we see things and how we treat other people.

I think if we feel pretty good about ourselves, we can usually handle just about anything that comes along without too much hassle. With your help, of course.

I don't think I would go as far as to say that I'm really "enjoying" my problems, but on the other hand, they don't seem as big to me as I once thought they were either.

You know when Ms. Wilson told us that you will never give us more than we can handle? Well, Pastor Hardy told us the same thing last Sunday, so it must be true. Boy, that really takes a load off my mind just knowing that.

He also told us that everything really belongs to you and that we're just stewards of everything here on earth. If I look at it that way, then when I tithe my ten percent, I'm really just giving back to you some of what you've already given me.

Do you know what else he said? He reminded us that you like to be appreciated the same way we do, so it's important to talk to you a lot and remember to thank you for things. I've been doing that a lot more lately, but I could probably do it even more than I am.

Then he ended his sermon with two questions for us to ask ourselves and think about. "What do I expect from God?" and "What does God expect from me?"

I guess I've never thought much about what you expect from me.

As far as what I expect from you: I expect you to love me unconditionally and to always be there for me. I expect you to be patient with me while I make all my mistakes and to forgive me when I ask you to and I tell you that I'm truly sorry. And I expect you to listen to my prayers and my problems and to help me when I need help.

I'm not sure what you expect from me. You probably hope that I'll listen to you when you try to guide me and that I'll always keep my faith and trust you even when bad things happen. And I know you want me to be a good steward of everything you have given us, especially the earth and the water and all the animals. Remember, I'm taking care of two of your white rats and Max, so don't forget to count them.

I know that you want me to live my life by the Ten Commandments, even though some kids I know don't think those are even valid anymore.

We talked about the Ten Commandments in one of our life groups and we decided that they make life easier for us, not harder. That's because you know the kinds of things that can get us in trouble.

And I think you also would like me to remember to tell you how much I love you too.

Boy, Pastor Hardy's questions really make you think, don't they? I think I may have to think a lot more about them over the summer.

Well, I guess I'll go call Jasmine and Megan and tell them the good news about Munch and Scrunch.

Dynamically yours,
Your friend, Leslie

P.S. I just thought of something. How do you think Max will look at Munch and Scrunch? As friends or as delectable "edibles"?

Dear God,

Well, my last day of my first year of junior high is finally here and I made it! Thanks to you and Ms. Wilson. Actually, I call her Laurie now and I've asked to be in her cabin at our youth camp this summer.

And thanks for taking care of Angelita for me. I finally found her last week in the box with Mom's angel figurines and she survived the move just fine.

I've got to tell you what a great friend you have been all year. You've always been there when I needed you. You've never criticized me or told me how dumb I was even though you must have thought it plenty of times.

You've been a terrific listener. You've always listened even when some of the things I told you probably *were* dumb. And you've never told anyone else any of my secrets which is really cool. Do you know how hard it is to find a friend you can really trust with your secrets?

To be honest, there were times when I really hoped you would do some things you didn't do. But what you did do was usually better than what I wanted you to do, so I learned to trust that you would always do what was best for me. You know, that "larger picture" again.

By not giving me everything I asked for exactly when I asked for it, I had to try to work some things out for myself. You knew all the time that that's what was best for me, didn't you? I guess that's how we all grow.

I've learned some important things this year. I've learned that you are real and that I can always count on you to be there for me. I guess the bottom line here is that I really have learned to trust you in everything and for everything.

And I've also learned that I am more together than I thought I was and that I can really count on myself too. I know now that I can trust myself to always do what I know in my heart is right.

And all that positive thinking stuff has been a big help too. I just can't believe how important your attitude is. What you think is going to happen usually does happen, so you might just as well think that good things are going to happen because then they probably will. I guess what I'm saying here is that it's important to focus on the good stuff and not the bad stuff.

I think I'm feeling strong enough now, so that even if Mom and Dad do go through with their divorce, I'll be okay. For a while there, I wasn't so sure, but now I am sure.

With your help and with my new positive attitude, how can I lose!

Victoriously yours,
Your *forever friend,* Leslie

P.S. I love you! A lot!